BRINGING

HEAVEN

DOWN TO EARTH

BRINGING
HEAVEN
DOWN TO EARTH

CONNECTING THIS LIFE TO THE NEXT

NATHAN L. K. BIERMA

P U B L I S H I N G

P.O. BOX 817 • PHILLIPSBURG • NEW JERSEY 08865-0817

"Morning Person" by Vassar Miller, from *Struggling to Swim on Concrete*, used with permission of New Orleans Poetry Journal Press.

Unless otherwise indicated, all Scripture quotations are from the HOLY BIBLE, NEW INTERNATIONAL VERSION®. NIV®. Copyright © 1973, 1978, 1984 by International Bible Society. Used by permission of Zondervan Publishing House. All rights reserved.

Italics within Scripture quotations indicate emphasis added.

Page design and typesetting by Lakeside Design Plus

Printed in the United States of America

Library of Congress Cataloging-in-Publication Data

Bierma, Nathan L. K., 1979–
    Bringing heaven down to earth : connecting this life to the next / Nathan L. K. Bierma.
        p. cm.
    Includes bibliographical references (p.) and index.
    ISBN-10: 0-87552-348-X (paper)
    ISBN-13: 978-087552-348-4 (paper)
        1. Christian life. 2. Future life. 3. Heaven. I. Title.

BV4501.3.B49 2005
248.4—dc22

                                            2005048865

51 Shalom defined
52-53
73
177-8
92
149 6-step process

CONTENTS

ACKNOWLEDGMENTS

This book has been gestating for ten years and amounts to a personal statement of the faith I've been cultivating during that time. The four most (and foremost) influential writers and thinkers who have shaped the ideas of this book are Richard Mouw, Neal Plantinga, Quentin Schultze, and Bill Romanowski. I hope the imprint of their influence is clear, and I hope my digressions from their writings are sound.

The wisdom, warmth, and energy of John Witvliet of the Calvin Institute of Christian Worship have been an inspiration and a blessing. The fellowship and collaboration with my other CICW colleagues is enjoyable and enriching. Many of my teachers, especially my professors at Calvin College and Chicago Semester, challenged and nourished me as a student, and some of them, such as Jim Vanden Bosch and Dale Brown, are now among my most cherished colleagues. The worship and preaching of Neland Avenue and Eastern Avenue Christian Reformed Churches in Grand Rapids and Fourth Presbyterian and LaSalle

Street Churches in Chicago have shaped my thinking and fed my faith.

I am indebted to John Wilson of *Books & Culture*, a gracious and erudite editor, and Lilah Lohr of the *Chicago Tribune*, an exacting editor and enthusiastic reader.

I am grateful to Al Fisher, Barbara Lerch, and Thom Notaro of P&R Publishing for their willingness to publish this book, and for their encouragement and guidance.

The friendship of Nathan VanderKlippe and Michael Sider-Rose has been a taste of heavenly fellowship, in moments of gravity and frivolity.

My family—Dad, Mom, and Lisa—have modeled for me compassion, curiosity, and a restlessness for the renewal of creation. My mother-in-law, Chris, and her husband, Randy, have truly become extended family. I wish Grandpa Bierma could have read this book; he has now gained special insight into the "in-between" state of fellowship with Christ, but eagerly awaits eternity. As does Watse.

My wife, Andrea, has taught me more than anyone else what heavenly "us-ness" is. She is my toughest critic and closest fellow sojourner.

My thanks to God is as follows.

LOST IN THE CORNFIELD

Hope in Crisis

enry David Thoreau lay on his deathbed. His good friend,
Parker Pillsbury, leaned over where he lay.

"David," he whispered, "do you have any vision of things
beyond?"

"One world at a time, Parker," Thoreau replied. "One world
at a time."

The purpose of this book is to show that Thoreau was dead
wrong.

Theologian Lewis Smedes once asked a room full of people
how many of them wanted to go to heaven. They all raised their

hands. Then he asked how many of them wanted to go to heaven that day. A couple of people cautiously raised their hands, nervously looking around to see if they were alone. They were.

Would you have raised your hand the second time? Would you want to go to heaven today, to experience heavenly existence before the sun sets? And would you want to stay?

Heaven is an odd element of the Christian faith. We profess it to be eternally important and then live as though it doesn't exist. We are runners who fear the finish line. We go through life with little sense of what heaven will be like, and less sense of why we would want to live there. We carry on with our lives, fixated on the here and now, oblivious to the there and then. The possibility of thinking about heaven on a daily basis—much less hoping for it to come—is washed away in the torrent of the details of daily life.

When you stop and think about it, this is a strange way to live. Heaven is so glorious, and the expanse of eternity so vast, it is a wonder we do not let our minds wander into its mysteries more often, and recognize its reality even in the most mundane moments of our lives. C. S. Lewis said we are like a child who would rather play in a sandbox than dream of the beach. Why is that? Why let a moment pass in this current life, this brief episode of history, without considering the everlasting existence that lies ahead? Why are we so shy?

Think of it, says Philip Yancey, as a math problem. "Although percentages don't apply to heaven, assume for the sake of argument that 99 percent of our existence will take place in heaven," he says. "Isn't it bizarre that we simply ignore heaven, acting as if it doesn't matter?"

We are indeed 1-percent people. The afterlife will reach to infinity, swallowing time, rendering our current age an infinitesimal blip on the cosmic timeline. This life will prove to be but the clearing of the throat before a song that never stops. Isn't it backwards, then, how much we concentrate on our tiny 1 percent? The other 99 percent may as well be a dream.

When I lived in Chicago and took the subway each morning, I would see people on a silent march from here to there, keeping pace with the ticking of an unseen clock. A steady stream of people would fill the subway—old bankers with briefcases, young women in business suits, weary college students clutching book bags, bleary-eyed teenagers with headphones ramming noise through their heads. I would mix among them all and march up the stairs of the subway station in silence, our feet pounding a rhythm on the stone stairs. Each of us was following some small destiny—the personal drama of a job to be done, classes to take, people to meet, accomplishments to achieve, failures to endure, all wrapped into the space of that day.

As we stepped together, none of us marchers knew the destiny of the next. We would view each other without warmth, march without passion, and, more often than not, go on to live without inspiration. Something seemed to be missing. Our steps landed too heavily. "You can tell," said the *Chicago Tribune*, "by the glum faces of the folks gobbling lunch at their desks, the ones morosely leaning against the coffee machine wondering how to get everything done by tonight, the walking workplace wounded, the folks who sit strangely hushed as they ride home, bone-tired, soul deflated, job not done, more of the same on the horizon."

Our society whirs on the motor of a small dream: that technological progress will bring us bliss. But our march continues in despond, this bliss ever elusive, the purpose of our march ever fuzzier. Our bargain with technology, writes Juliet Schor, was a bust. Our commitment to capitalism was supposed to

3

buy us time, buy us leisure, buy us balance, and most of all, buy us happiness. But we are empty. We march so hard in pursuit of this promise that it only feels farther away. With every new technological advance, it seems we need more time to use it. With every innovation in communications, it's harder to communicate with people. Leisure, writes Schor, is a "conspicuous casualty of prosperity."

But if prosperity is no longer our goal, and leisure is not our true destiny, why do we keep marching? What is the engine that drives us day after day?

I used to imagine stopping people in the subway tunnel and asking them if they ever thought about heaven. I never dared. I figured I would draw blank looks or a curt dismissal. *Newsweek* reports that 76 percent of Americans say they believe in heaven; 71 percent agree with the description that heaven is "an actual place." The *New York Times* notes that belief in the afterlife has increased since the 1970s, even as church attendance has declined. But heaven is not a topic on which many people dwell, especially not on the noisy subway.

The promise of heaven is meant to place our lives in a larger context, to fix us to a firmer foundation than the thin dreams of today's society, to give us hope. So why is hope for the afterlife not a heartfelt reality in our daily walk? Why do we ignore eternity and live as though it isn't coming anytime soon, and that it doesn't have anything to do with what we're doing now?

In North America, Christians are in crisis. This crisis reaches to all areas of our lives and makes it hard for us to be satisfied and inspired in anything but superficial and sentimental ways.

We have a crisis of hope.

We live without a deep sense of ultimate meaning, broader purpose, or eternal destiny. We proceed with our daily duties without a vision for why we're doing them. We go to school, start a business, grow a family, buy a house, take a job, go to church. All of these things make up our personal stories. But rarely do we try to place them in a larger story.

We have a shortage of hope. We may have desires and cravings for food, sex, and other pleasures. We may have allegiances to sports teams or political causes and would like to see their success. We may have optimism about our future at school or the office. We may live with anticipation of future milestones in our lives—graduations, weddings, births, anniversaries. But rarely do we live with *hope*, true hope—the combination of the assurance of God's ultimate triumph over evil, the comfort of an eventual eternal, misery-free existence, and the longing for Christ to come again to bring this about. We are not filled with a visceral, vital hope for heaven that seeps into every crevice of our souls and transforms our daily lives.

"If it is hope that maintains and upholds faith and keeps it moving on, if it is hope that draws the believer into the life of love," writes Jurgen Moltmann in *Theology of Hope*, "then it will also be hope that is the mobilizing and driving force of faith's thinking, of its knowledge of, and reflections on, human nature, history, and society." The lack of hope, Moltmann says, is a sin—a rejection of the abundance God's promise, a timidity to live with God's passion, purpose, and direction. Or, as Smedes says more bluntly, "The person without hope is inwardly dead."

But in our crisis of hope, we focus on what is immediately in front of us. We live in the short term. Every once in a while, a Sunday morning church service or the funeral of a loved one may shake us into an awareness of the coming of eternal heaven. But we quickly retreat into our ordinary routines. We make what the poet John Keats called "the journey homeward to habitual self." We fail to stay in a constant state of anticipation, the

5

trance of the fascinating idea that this world is only a brief prologue to the one to come. Hope is not our constant context.

As a result, the word *heaven* is becoming inoperative in contemporary Christianity. If we keep pushing it to the edges of our periphery and emptying it of meaning, sooner or later it will be worthless. "Like classic cars, some words need to be restored," says Arthur Roberts in *Exploring Heaven*. "*Heaven* is one such word."

Part of the problem is that we associate going to heaven with death. Heaven happens to old people when they wither and die, we think, or to younger people when their lives are tragically cut short. In a society that worships youth and fears aging, death is defeat, and heaven is meager compensation.

But the main causes of our crisis of hope for heaven are more profound. As I see it, there are two. First, we don't know what heaven will be like. Second, we don't know when Christ will return and unveil eternity. How can we hope for such an unknown quantity?

The truth is, we cannot know now exactly what heaven will be like, and we cannot know exactly when it will come. But if we are going to lead lives tinged with hope and driven by anticipation, we must get a sense of what heaven has to do with the lives we live, the natural world we encounter, the society we are a part of, and the timeline that human existence follows like a ribbon into eternity. We must rediscover what the promise of heaven is and how it is relevant to every area of life. Without this connection, our empty march will go on; our crisis of hope will only get worse.

North American Christians find themselves in a peculiar place in history. We live under some of the most powerful governments in the world in an era of unprecedented prosperity, with a quality of life that makes medieval kings look like peasants. And yet we are empty, deflated by the despair of personal failure and spiritual disorientation, discouraged by the evil and uncertainty around the world and next door. And so, in the midst of the proudest society humankind has ever brought about, we have an alarming deficit of hope. We are so depleted now that nations we had been sending missionaries to for centuries, in Asia and Africa, have now caught spiritual fire and are sending their own missionaries back to North America.

What does it mean to live as a Christian under these circumstances? What does it mean for the church to exist and to bless a continent blighted by this crisis of hope? How do we rediscover what hope is and begin to hope again? How do we tether ourselves to hope's anchor, the promise of eternal heaven? How do we lose our shyness about talking about heaven and gain the confidence to know enough about it to want it? How do we rediscover that the earth we inhabit and the things we make in its midst are part of a larger cosmic story, of which God pens every stroke? How can we begin to sketch a basic framework that encompasses our lives, our earth and society, history and the future, and from this framework find deeper meaning?

These questions have consumed me since, after being reared in a religious home and a church-laced community, I first encountered the truth of the biblical picture of heaven in high school, in a book called *When the Kings Come Marching In* by Richard Mouw. His interpretation of the prophet Isaiah's vision of the heavenly city so altered my assumptions and ignited my thinking that I lost some of my shyness about the subject. I have since come to believe Christians are missing out on a major sense of purpose by having too small and too distant a view of heaven.

Foolish as it would be to try to improve on Dr. Mouw's work, and unreasonable to demand he defend my digressions from it, I do hope to call Christians to take a new look at Dr. Mouw's ideas by tying them more explicitly to John's vision of heaven in Revelation 21, from the standpoint of a journalist. As I found out, adjusting our picture of heaven means undoing some heavily enforced learning. But any small measure of success opens the possibility of living with a new sense of hope and meaning.

Ultimately, heaven remains a mystery, a foreign realm that has no natives save for the angels and the glorious presence of God. And so there are a lot of good reasons not to think about heaven very much. But there are even better reasons why we should.

In the series finale of the sit-com *SportsNight*, Dana, a television producer, takes her worries to a Manhattan bar, where she encounters a friendly stranger. The stranger listens to Dana as she spills her fears. When she finishes, he says, "Dana, I'm what the world considers to be a phenomenally successful man, and I've failed much more than I've succeeded. But each time I fail, I get my people together, and I say, 'Where are we going?', and it starts to get better. And that's what you should do." His company, she learns, is called Quo Vadimus, which is Latin for "Where are we going?"

Christians need to ask the same question. We need to get our people together and say, Where are we going? Where does this all end? What's the point? To give meaning to the ongoing drama of history, we need a healthy new look at how history ends. To rediscover the meaning of the present, we need to unlock the secrets of the future. Somehow, some way, we need to have hope for heaven.

Heads in the Clouds

Follow an empty dirt road out of the tiny town of Dyersville, Iowa, until you find yourself in the middle of nowhere. Keep tracing the endless rows of corn until you round a bend and see a startling sight: the neatly trimmed lawn and golden sand of a baseball field. Stadium lights sprout from telephone poles surrounding the field like sentries, and nearby stands a white farmhouse. Each year, thousands of people make this pilgrimage to the farm of Don Lansing, where the movie *Field of Dreams* was filmed. Lansing maintains the field for the crowds of tourists. Many of them run around the bases and snap photographs of his famous farmhouse.

In the movie, Ray, played by Kevin Costner, hears a whispering voice from the sky that inspires him to build a baseball diamond in his cornfield. When he builds the field, the ghost of baseball legend Shoeless Joe Jackson appears on it at night. Soon Shoeless Joe is joined by other baseball greats who materialize as they walk out from the corn stalks in the outfield. Today, tourists instruct family members to take their pictures among the same corn stalks, ambling out in the manner of the movie's phantoms.

When Shoeless Joe first appears in the movie, his eyes widen as he surveys the emerald field and the sparkling sand.

"Hey," he shouts to Ray. "Is this heaven?"

"No," Ray chuckles. "It's Iowa."

Ray's memorable reprimand aside, the idyllic setting of this magical baseball field contributes to our imagination of what heaven will be like. The scene of baseball players playing their beloved game on this field apart from time, without a care in the world on the tranquil Iowan plain, makes Shoeless Joe's question eerily resonant for the thousands of tourists who travel to Dyersville each summer. They are transfixed by their encounter with an unknown world.

Because we know so little about what heaven will be like, we seize upon poignant images and icons like the *Field of Dreams* farm in Dyersville to give us a hint. We may not think about heaven that much, but when we do, we take our cues from the images of paintings, hymns, and popular culture. We tend to pay little attention to the theological work we let them do for us. As evangelical pollster George Barna told the *Dallas Morning News*, "Many Americans adopt simplistic views of life and the afterlife based upon ideas drawn from disparate sources, such as movies, music, and novels, without carefully considering those beliefs."

Despite their vagaries, our images of heaven are some of the most beautiful scenes known to human beings. One of the most vivid portrayals of heaven on film is another movie with dreams in the title: *What Dreams May Come*. When the main character, played by Robin Williams, is killed, his first vision of the afterlife is the living world of the paintings of his wife, an artist. He walks into a picturesque setting that resembles her scenic landscapes and awesome vistas. He dives off a steep cliff, tumbles over a waterfall down thousands of feet of sheer rock, and lands comfortably in a flowerbed. As he walks, the grass and flowers beneath his feet squish and smear; they are made of his wife's paint. He laughs as he turns and surveys a world that stretches as far he can see, to an elusive horizon beyond canyons and lakes, as the sun streams down all around him. Our own imagination of heaven may resemble this wondrous realm.

Another way we imagine heaven is as a place where we get everything we want, the perfect fulfillment of our greatest indulgences. We suppose that if we could play golf all day long, or eat ceaseless supplies of chocolate without a care, or go on vacation and never come back, we would be in seventh heaven or on cloud nine.

The things we see and read feed this idea. I signed on to America Online recently and was greeted by a picture of a luscious piece of raspberry cream pie. Next to it was the headline, "What Heaven Must Taste Like." I opened my *New Yorker* and found a special advertising section urging readers to vacation in the Dominican Republic. One resort said that while the whole island nation is beautiful, "the real paradise here is Punta Cana Resort and Club, where [various celebrities] have all built their Caribbean vacation homes." This appeared alongside another advertisement that blithely proclaimed, "Heaven Can Wait."

We also rely on portrayals of heaven based, however loosely, on the Bible. The most common scene in popular culture is the sight of Saint Peter standing in front of the pearly gates, admitting people into heaven. In the comic strip "Frank & Earnest," the two characters are perched on a puffy cloud before a kindly old Peter, his wings jutting out the back of his white robe, a halo hovering over his forehead. He stands before a podium that bears a thick book while light rays pulse from a grand gate behind him. A sign by the gate reads, "New Arrivals Stop Here For Admissions Processing." In the comic strip's punch line, one of the characters pleads, "Don't ask me any tough questions— I left my brain to Harvard."

In a commercial for a candy bar, people wait in line on a long cloud to pass through Peter's heavenly checkpoint. One would-be entrant is taking a while with Saint Peter, and a man farther back shouts that they should hurry things along. In an instant the man plunges through the cloud, presumably on his way to hell. (The message of the ad was to eat a candy bar when you have a long wait.)

Peter's benediction in a cartoon printed on a greeting card I saw seems to sum up our expectations: "Welcome to heaven," he says. "Here's your harp." (The joke was that people in hell got accordions.) Many of us have come to expect that Peter will indeed greet us this way when we get to the pearly gates.

Sacred hymns, seizing on images from the Gospels and the Book of Revelation, spin out these fantastic visions even further:

> By the sea of crystal saints in glory stand,
> myriads in number drawn from every land.
> Robed in white apparel, washed in Jesus' blood,
> they now reign in heaven with the Lamb of God.

And:

> In mansions of glory and endless delight,
> I'll ever adore thee in heaven so bright.
> I'll sing with a glittering crown on my brow,
> "If ever I loved thee, my Jesus, 'tis now."

All of these fantasies may leave us with a heartwarming but rather vague sense of the afterlife. As pleasant as they are, these pictures are not enough to inspire us to hope for eternal heaven on a daily basis. Heaven, we gather, is an airy and serene existence among clouds and meadows, where we wear robes and strum harps. It is peaceful and quiet. Maybe too quiet.

Many of us are in no hurry to hear Peter tell us, "Welcome to heaven. Here's your harp." When I e-mailed my friend Nathan, who shares not only my name but also my vocation as a newspaper reporter, and I told him about my idea for this book, he asked some of his colleagues about what they thought of heaven. He e-mailed me back and paraphrased what they said.

"They told me flat-out that they simply didn't want to go to heaven. Who wants in to a place with twenty-four-hour harp Muzak and hallelujah choruses on the quarter hour from here to wherever infinity takes us? I'd rather be mortal."

I was surprised to read that C. S. Lewis says something similar. Noting that the Bible decorates heaven with "palms, crowns, white robes, [and] thrones," he comments, "The natural appeal of this authoritative imagery is to me, at first, very small. At first sight it chills, rather than awakes, my desire."

But Lewis goes on to say that the way we have adopted these heavenly images is fraught with mistakes. The first problem is that the biblical images we use are actually metaphors for beauty, happiness, and wholeness, and we distort their meanings when we take them too literally. The clouds, the meadows, the harps—all of these are meant only to hint at the perfect gladness of being with God in heaven. Although we have every reason to believe that heaven will contain natural beauty and music, these biblical images are not snapshots of heavenly locations. J. Nelson Kraybill makes a good point in comparing the writing styles of John and Paul in the New Testament: "Instead of using logical argument and deductive reasoning like Paul the apostle, John uses pictures and narrative to convey his inspired message. Think symbol. Think metaphor. Think poetry. Don't get trapped with wooden literalism—unless you really expect to get to heaven and find that Jesus is a sheep."

So we should not get carried away. The idea of pearly gates, for example, comes from the Book of Revelation, where heaven is portrayed as having twelve gates, one for each of the twelve apostles. Each base of the gate is made of a different kind of precious stone, and the gates themselves are made of pearls. The number twelve stands for completeness, and the pearls sig-

nify splendor and durability. Many of our other heavenly fix-
tures—such as angels, robes, and harps—also come from the
last book of the Bible. But we must be careful how much we
embellish these heavenly symbols in our movies, cartoons,
hymns, and imaginations. We must realize that, by themselves,
these pictures cannot convey such a blissful existence. This is
how Lewis explains it:

> Musical instruments are mentioned because for many people
> (not all) music is the thing known in the present life which
> most strongly suggests ecstasy and infinity. . . . Gold is men-
> tioned to suggest the timelessness of Heaven (gold does not
> rust) and the preciousness of it. People who take these sym-
> bols literally might as well think that when Christ told us to
> be like doves, He meant that we were to lay eggs.

When we take these things too literally, they turn out to be
not much to hope for. The heaven they foreshadow may seem
like a nice vacation—who wouldn't want to lounge around in a
tropical paradise after a hard week at the office?—but they do
not give us a heavenly promise we can seize and implant in our
hearts to change our lives. They are not a very welcoming vision
of our permanent residence. Is heaven just a nice place to visit,
or would we really want to live there?

Heaven is not a never-never land skirted by clouds. When
we realize this, and when we re-imagine what heaven will be
like, we can begin to truly hope for heaven rather than keep
our anxious distance from it. Revising our heavenly visions
by taking a closer look at what those biblical metaphors mean
can allow us to live with a meaningful vision of the afterlife.
We need to look past the pearly gates at what really lies behind
them.

False Alarms

The announcement said to mark your calendar for Wednesday, October 28, 1992. A chart listed the time for major cities around the world: 10 a.m. in New York. Three in the afternoon in London. Four o'clock in Rome. Midnight in Tokyo. And there was no mistaking the urgency of the notice.

"**RAPTURE**," read the flyer across the top in bold capital letters. "**OCTOBER 28, 1992, JESUS IS COMING IN THE AIR.**" Beneath this banner headline was a Bible verse: "Fear God, and give him glory, because the hour of his judgment has come" (Rev. 14:7). This banner's "**TIMETABLE OF RAPTURE**" pinned down the minute of doomsday for each time zone. Above it was a chaotic picture of a cityscape. Cars lay askew along the side of freeways, their drivers, looking like white tadpoles swimming upstream, floated heavenward with their arms outstretched. The shimmering figure of Jesus appeared above it all as a magnet drawing the raptured souls to the sky. The flyer was distributed by the Mission for the Coming Days in Flushing, New York, and included the organization's logo and phone number.

But on October 29, 1992, the world kept spinning. People went about their business as they had on the 28th, and the 27th before that. The rapture warning was a false alarm. Life on earth went on.

It's hard to hope for heaven because we don't know when Christ will come back and usher in the rest of eternity. He could come in a second, in an hour, or in a millennium or three. So eternal heaven is a mystery for its time of arrival. The trumpet could blast at any minute, or it could be silent for another century. Jesus could return before you finish this chapter, before the week is out, or long after you're cold in the grave. What an awkward way to live. Our eternal destiny, 1 Thessalonians 5 tells us, will come "like a thief in the night," which sounds more like a threat than a promise.

In a soccer match, the clock ticks steadily until it reaches ninety minutes. At that point the referee takes out his personal stopwatch and counts the minutes he or she estimates were lost at noncompetitive moments in the match. It may be two minutes; it may be four or more. The players proceed to play with no precise notion of when they will finish. Unlike basketball players, who keep an eye on the ticking clock as the final seconds wind down so that they can try a winning shot at the final buzzer, the soccer players play in a strange state of limbo. Then, all of a sudden, the referee blows the whistle, and the match is over, just like that.

Now imagine that the entire match is played by the referee's watch. Imagine that the players have no concept of temporal dimensions for the entirety of their playing time. The referee could blow the whistle seven minutes after kickoff or midway through the second half. No possibility is more likely than any other. What would it be like to play such an uneasy game? Would you run faster throughout the second half, as your anticipation of the end grew more acute? Or would you run as fast as you could the entire time, unwilling to let the whistle blow during anything but your fiercest effort?

This is the puzzle that surrounds us as we live. We have no concept of when time will run out, when the whistle will blow, when Jesus will return and interrupt life like a clap of thunder. We conceive of terms like *history* and *the future* while ignoring the larger book that gives them meaning—a story that has been building for thousands of years but will surely stop on a dime. We keep clocks, watches, and timepieces all around us but remain oblivious to the apocalyptic nature of time itself.

We find ourselves in the same state of uncertainty as the ten bridal attendants in Jesus' parable in Matthew 25. They went outside to wait for the arrival of the bride and groom at the wedding banquet, and each took an oil-burning lamp to help them keep watch. Five of them brought extra oil with them to keep handy in case the wait was long. The others did not, and they ran out of fuel before the bride and groom arrived. But while they were away, getting more oil, the couple came and the banquet began. The five latecomers tried to enter, but they were turned away. "Keep your lamps trimmed and burning," intones the spiritual. "The time is drawing nigh."

Instead, we are content to live short-sightedly. We choose the most comfortable way to adjust to the odd reality that existence could be suspended at any second; we choose the path of least resistance. We lapse into complacency. We keep the second coming out of our minds. We live our lives from day to day, following our routines from sunrise to sunset. " 'Thy Kingdom come,' we pray," says Cornelius Plantinga, " 'but not right away.' " We make plans days and years in advance, without giving the impending trumpet a second thought. After all, "it's so full of emergency," Plantinga said, in a sermon I heard him preach when I was in college. So we try to reach a point of greater stability.

And who can blame us? Who can walk around with their heads in the clouds? Who can maintain the pose of the apostles, heads arched toward the sky as they watched Christ ascend and were told to wait for him to descend in the same way? Realistically, if we amble around with our eyes fixed to the heavens, we'll get sore necks, and we'll bump into things. As William Willimon puts it, "It's hard to stand on tiptoe for two thousand years." As we lose our sensation of the coming eternity, Plantinga says,

17

"people settle into a kind of 'everydayness' in their faith, and they quit scanning the horizon." It's a functional way to maintain our religion, if not a very powerful one.

The problem is that we're supposed to not only *expect* the earth-shattering suddenness of the second coming; we're supposed to *hope* for it. But how can we desire something so impossible to predict? It's one thing to hope for, say, the birth of a baby, which will happen in about nine months, or for graduation, whose month and day are settled upon enrollment, giving relatives enough time to book plane tickets. Even when you get a new job, you don't vanish from your old one; you give your boss two weeks' notice. So if the issue is making heaven a reality in every moment of our daily lives and avoiding complacency, we have to wonder: how can we naturally hope for something that will come so suddenly and yet hasn't come for hundreds of years?

To solve this problem, too many people have tried to crack the case of when Christ will return. Anne Lamott calls them "Christians who think that Jesus is coming back next Tuesday right after lunch." As the authors of *The New Millennium Manual* report, many have produced careful calculations, with impressive evidence, and formed a timetable for the second coming.

Third-century Roman theologian Hippolytus was one of the first to guess the date of Christ's return. He went through the Bible like a mathematician and calculated that Christ would come back in the year 500. But 500 came and went. Centuries later, Joachim in Fiore guessed that the date would be 1260, and throughout that year he paraded around with bands of men who beat themselves with whips, calling others to repentance. But 1260 came and went. Others thought the bubonic plague, the Black Death, signaled the end of the world, and so Bohemian monks set 1420 as the year of Christ's return. But 1420 came and went.

In 1836, William Miller published a book that forecasted a second coming for 1843. He developed quite a following of people, who are known today as the Seventh-day Adventists. Miller's followers didn't lose hope when 1843 came to an end; they set a new date: October 22, 1844. October 23 came to be known as "The Great Disappointment."

Charles Taze Russell, the founder of Jehovah's Witnesses, first predicted an apocalypse for 1873 or 1874. Then he said 1878, and then 1914, then 1918. In 1981, Bill Maupin of Tucson, Arizona, predicted the end of the world would come on June 28, 1982. A reporter asked him what would happen on June 29 if his forecast proved false. "I can't even answer a question like that," Maupin said. "Come back and see us on June 29 and we'll talk about it." June 28 came and went.

A few years later Edward Whisenant sold two million copies of his book, *88 Reasons Why the Rapture Could Be in 1988*. He predicted a second coming for September 11–13 of that year. One publishing company in Raleigh, North Carolina, was so taken by the book that it closed for the day on the 13th. The 13th came and went.

Then a pamphlet pronounced, "In Autumn 1992, Jesus is Coming! In 1999, Human History Will End!" The Mission for the Coming Days poster, with the raptured drivers floating to heaven, was more specific, setting the time as October 28 at ten in the morning. But of course 10 a.m., and the rest of the day, came and went. This didn't deter religious broadcaster Harold Camping, who wrote *1994* and *Are You Ready*. But New Year's Eve confetti sprang like Old Faithful in 1995.

The Y2K computer scare brought another massive wave of apocalyptic panic. Wrote a Jerusalem reporter in 1999, "Among those who are preparing for the Second Coming are about 100 evangelical North Americans who have moved to apartments on the Mount of Olives, for a close-up view of the prophesied return of Jesus." New Year's Day 2000 came and went.

Now a new movement is emerging: Exit 2007.

All these self-anointed prophets boldly ignore Christ's words that the time of his arrival is a bona fide unsolved mystery. "No one knows about that day or hour, not even the angels in heaven, nor the Son, but only the Father," he says in Matthew 24. These prophets are trying to win at a game that Christ chose not to play. Of course, they may claim that although we can't know the day or the hour, we can know the month and the week, but this violates the spirit, if not the letter, of Christ's words. These prophets have somehow found a greater emphasis in the Bible on the need to decipher prophecy than to wait in mystery.

After a while we become mindful of the story of the boy who cried wolf. As the story goes, the town appointed a boy to keep watch for wolf attacks on the town's flocks of sheep. One night, out of boredom, he awoke everyone with a desperate cry of "Wolf!" And the townspeople ran around in a panic, scrambling to protect their sheep. But there was no wolf. The second night, bored again, the boy did the same thing. But there was no wolf. The third night, a wolf actually came. But when the boy cried out "Wolf!" the townspeople were wise to what they thought was another game, and so they ignored the boy and stayed in bed. The wolf had its fill of lamb chops.

Although we must give doomsday prophets the benefit of the doubt about their intentions and not automatically assume that they are making a ruckus and getting people panicked simply for their own amusement or profit, we must also acknowledge the cumulative effect of their errors. Every time a rapture alert comes and goes, we pay less attention the next time. It's why few people are holding their breath for Exit 2007. After so many false alarms, we are no longer alarmed at all.

Plantinga coined a provocative phrase in his sermon about waiting for the second coming. He said that the majority of Christians respond to these fantastic guessing games by piously distancing themselves from any mention of the Book of Revelation and the end of the world. We're so embarrassed by these alarmist prophecies that we begin to neglect the second coming altogether. After all, this talk of the future is so exotic, but religion can be more predictable. "We've got *eschatological chastity*," Plantinga said. "We've got restraint." And we're proud of it.

But as we practice abstinence from the study of the last things, we also lose hope. We let time go by and push history's surprise ending out of our minds. We don't know when eternal heaven will come, so we let it go. Our crisis of hope gets worse.

So we miss out on the biggest piece of life's puzzle: the afterlife and what it means for our current life. "If people really understood the Christian promise of heaven, they'd be more excited about it and more inclined to try to get there," Anthony DeStefano, author of *A Travel Guide to Heaven*, told the *Dallas Morning News*. Lewis says the same thing in "The Weight of Glory," the most incredible sermon I have ever heard or read:

Indeed, if we consider the unblushing promises of reward and the staggering nature of the rewards promised in the Gospels, it would seem that Our Lord finds our desires, not too strong, but too weak. We are half-hearted creatures, fooling about with drink and sex and ambition when infinite joy is offered us, like an ignorant child who wants to go on making mud pies in a slum because he cannot imagine what is meant by the offer of a holiday at the sea. We are far too easily pleased.

So much for eschatological chastity. Our restraint around matters of the afterlife doesn't impress God. It disappoints God.

The truth is, we can do nothing to eliminate the two major causes of our crisis of hope—that we don't know what heaven will be like and we don't know when eternity will arrive. Although this book is about heaven, it will not—cannot—disclose what exactly heavenly living will be like or when the rest of eternity will begin. Christ said it himself: it's unknown.

But even though we shouldn't play guessing games about the second coming, it is a grievous mistake to ignore it. As many great preachers have said, the signs of the times do not tell us *when* Jesus is coming back, but they tell us *that* he is coming back. And they do so with a forcefulness that condemns the complacent act of simply pushing the promise of Christ's return out of our minds. We need to ask and answer the all-important question about our faith and our life: Where are we going?

We need to lose some of our eschatological chastity and trade it in for some eschatological *curiosity*—some healthy imagination about the coming of heaven and what it means for life now.

Until we second-guess and tweak our typical pictures of heaven, we will not let them inspire us as glimpses of the world toward which this one is building. We will not correct our crisis of hope. But by reexamining what the biblical message about heaven really is and painting a new picture of what it means for daily life, hope can be reborn.

ON PURPOSE

Meaning in Crisis

No sooner do two women enter the department store ahead of me than they are intercepted by a giddy greeter: "Ladies, give me thirty seconds to change the texture of your eyes forever." Upon their nods she seats them in chairs and begins dabbing their faces with whatever she's selling. Her cloth emits one of the many competing fragrances in the busy aisles around me. Outside, similar seductions are underway on this day after Thanksgiving along North Michigan Avenue in Chicago. A sign in the window of Banana Republic announces a drawing for a shopping spree it calls the "Win Your Every Wish Sweepstakes." A bus billboard advises, "Make Your Presents Felt." A boutique displays a crystal Nativity set in the window; inside I am told that the set of three wise men, poised in their worship of a penniless King, sells for one thousand dollars.

The day after Thanksgiving has become nearly as much of a national holiday in America as its predecessor. It was of enough importance to command the attention of U.S. President Franklin D. Roosevelt in 1939, as he paused from pondering a depression and world war to decree that Thanksgiving be moved up that year from the 30th to the 23rd, so as to extend the shopping season. Ever since, we've been hurrying our thanks and indulging our material appetites, allowing gratitude to give way, literally overnight, to gratification.

Here on Michigan Avenue in Chicago, with its row of major retailers and its nickname "the Magnificent Mile," this pursuit can resemble a stampede. Though the sidewalks are wide, progress along them is slow today, as the mass of shoppers swells and occasionally comes to a standstill. I fall in behind two girls in their early teens with purses on their arms and a bounce in their step, but men and women of all ages and races are out and about today. "Oh, man, it's been nuts," says the greeter at a shoe retailer when I ask him how the day is going. I pass two shouting saleswomen trying to shove slips of paper into the hands of passersby. I take one and read its plea to shop over the Internet. "Are you a Shop Lunatic?" it asks me. I look around and conclude that, given my decision to traverse these streets today, the answer would have to be yes.

Inside the Disney store, I begin to make a list of items bearing the image of Mickey Mouse. I lose count after finding a plush toy, snow globe, toaster, umbrella, slippers, and model airplane with Mickey's mug. I find myself murmuring along to the cooing track of "Joy to the World" overhead: "Let earth receive her king. . . . He rules the world with truth and grace."

Humming this awkward invocation, I idle in front of the Disney princess castle play set, examining the pink spires sprinkled with glitter. As I turn to the wall-length shelves bearing princess accessories—purses, clothes, and carriages—I wonder what the two have to do with each other: that song and this stuff, the Prince of Peace and the Disney princess. What does that glittering castle have to do with the one who "rules the world with truth and grace"?

Never in history has a society been so filled with and fixated on *things* as in North America today. More and more, our lives consist of material goods, from the car we drive to the clothes we wear to the appliances we use and the entertainment devices with which we occupy ourselves. For the first time in the history of economics, shopping has become a recreational activity, something we do for fun. We spend more and more time using and shopping for gadgets and garments and less and less time interacting with people and building meaningful relationships.

Anna Quindlen, columnist and self-described shopaholic, confessed during a recent holiday season, "For this recovering shopper, right now the ads, the catalogs, the stores all feel more like hallmarks of an addiction than an indulgence." But she said she'd made a breakthrough: "I do not need an alpaca swing coat, a tourmaline brooch, a mixer with a dough hook, a CD player that works in the shower, another pair of boot-cut black pants, lavender bath salts, vanilla candles or a Kate Spade Gucci Prada Coach bag." But if the Magnificent Mile is any indication, not everyone has Quindlen's newly found restraint.

Even the neighborhoods we live in have become communities of consumers. In the past, neighborhoods would coalesce among people who shared common beliefs, traditions, or ethnic histories. Today, all that most neighbors have in common are their real estate purchases—the comparable prices they paid for their houses. We have evolved from neighborly neighborhoods to suburbs of strangers. Our neighbors are our neighbors because they are consumers, and so are we.

But has this preponderance of purchases made anyone any happier? Never before have so many material wants been met so freely and quickly, and yet the result seems merely to be more wants. We have a chronic concern for our commodities, an anxiety about the acquisition of things. It is like a disease, say the authors of the book *Affluenza: The All-Consuming Epidemic.* They define the affluenza virus as a "condition of overload, debt, anxiety and waste resulting from the dogged pursuit of more." *More* proves inexhaustible. People overextend their means to buy things and sink into debt. Credit card debt has suddenly become a social crisis. In the United States, says Juliet Schor, cases of personal bankruptcy leapt from 200,000 in 1980 to 1.4 million less than twenty years later.

People who defend the consumptive imperative of capitalism point out that no one is forced to buy anything and that consumer choice is a great triumph of individual freedom. This glosses over some troubling facts about materialism. Buying is often an irrational and random act, not rational and deliberate. Schor notes that shoppers are, inexplicably, more likely to turn right than left when they enter a store, and they are less likely to buy products placed in the first several paces of a store's entrance. Marketers, meanwhile, clearly see shoppers not as calculating people seeking to make a rational choice but as vulnerable to seduction by glitzy ads and talk of magic and wishes.

That talk—so prevalent on this day after Thanksgiving—is instructive. It makes the act of buying more than just a matter of meeting a need or want; it has a spiritual dimension, or, more accurately, an antispiritual dimension. The more we rely on material goods to satisfy our desires, the less sustenance we receive from spiritual sources. The suspicion of many social theorists, who note that the rise of mass consumption coincided with the decline of traditional religious communities, is that we are filling our lives with things because our lives are emptier than they once were; we are less connected to other people and groups, less anchored by communal understandings of religious meaning. "The hopes and dreams people once sought to realize through systems of traditional religious symbols and the institutions associated with them," writes historian Jon Pahl in *Shopping Malls and Other Sacred Spaces*, "are now sought through economic accumulation and status display and by shopping at the most fashionable malls."

Malls themselves have come to fulfill sacred functions. Churches were once the focal points of neighborhoods and travelers; now malls are. Pahl says the way malls make use of light, ceilings, trees, fountains, and music is comparable to the way churches use those physical features in their buildings. Their atmosphere assumes supernatural qualities. The psalmist gazed at the stars in wonder; on the Magnificent Mile, the array of twinkling lights suspended in the trees along the sidewalk resemble stars in a pseudo-sky slung low over the heads of shoppers. The cosmetics greeter I overheard claimed to work wonders— nothing less than to "change the texture of your eyes forever." She viewed her ceremony the way some believers view baptism: the application of a holy substance to the body to bring about eternal transformation.

But materialism cannot satisfy the soul. Chasing the ephemeral sensations provided by purchasing things we urgently want but will quickly abandon is an empty endeavor. Pahl cautions Christians not to "conform to marketed symbols of 'beauty' or marketed commodities as signs of the 'good' life," since, he says, "their primary damage is to the human heart and mind." This cycle of consumption, this material madness, surely speaks to a deeper spiritual searching among people living in a confusing age, taking up a dance with the fleeting as a diversion from the lasting.

The problem is not only how malls and shopping serve sacred purposes—or rather, serve as shallow substitutes for sacred things—but also how our preoccupation with the material numbs us to the reality of the immaterial, the transcendent, the eternal. Materialism trains us on the moment, the passing desire, the good that will soon be gone when we want something else. Sellers do not want buyers to be mindful of eternity, since eternity is a distraction from our passing desires and thus a threat to their profits.

While there is nothing inherently wrong with material goods, as we will see in chapter 4, our relationship with, passion for, and acquisition of these things can quickly become unhealthy habits for believers who are supposed to be on a spiritual journey. Our obsession with comfort and prosperity is inconsistent with the Bible's call to be selfless, suffering servants. Malcolm Muggeridge said he came to realize that our modern-day "exercises in self-gratification" amount to "diversions designed to distract our attention from the true purpose of our existence in this world, which is, quite simply, to look for God, and, in looking, to find him, and having found him, to love him, thereby establishing a harmonious relationship with his purposes for creation." Our quest is not for acquisition but for harmony.

Before North Americans got so caught up in *things*, our lives tended to revolve around our relationship to the land, to God, and to each other. With this could come a spiritual vibrancy and a realization of mortality, of the brevity of life, prompting eternal questions about the unseen. Today we focus much more on the concrete and immediate, and the result is often spiritual vacuousness. The more that material goods come to define our existence in—and relationship to—the world, and the more our lives are defined by what we can see and feel and obtain, the more we desire the finite, the immediate, the now—and the more we become numb to infinity, the larger picture of cosmic history, the coming of heaven. James Twitchell sums it up perfectly: "When we have few things, we make the next world holy. When we have plenty, we enchant the objects around us."

The proliferation of consumption has not fully dissolved our deeper questions about life and about heaven. Schor says most North Americans "struggle with ongoing conflicts between materialism and an alternative set of values stressing family, religion, community, social commitment, equity, and personal meaning," and that they desire "an alternative vision of a quality of life, rather than a quantity of stuff." In a sermon at Fourth Presbyterian Church on the Magnificent Mile in Chicago, the Reverend John Buchanan reported the results of a study of American consumption. "What [the study] found was surprising," Buchanan said. "Most people knew that money can't buy happiness. Only healthy reciprocal relationships can do that. What most people want is abundant life, full, meaningful, happy lives and that they are asking essentially the greatest question in the world, 'How do I get that?' " Even as we fill our lives with things, we know that what we really want to be filled with is hope and meaning.

An earnest exploration of the question How do I get that? loosens our attachment to things, our entanglement in constant gratification and wanton wanting. Freedom from these anxieties enables us to find transcendent truth, and begins a more fulfilling search for what will last, for where we are going, for the truth of eternity. We are drawn away from the finite by the infinite and drawn nearer to the reality of heaven.

Monotony of Meaninglessness

"The question remains: What are we going to do now?" says Lelaina, wrapping up her pessimistic graduation speech in the 1994 movie *Reality Bites.* "How can we repair all the damage we inherited? Fellow graduates, the answer is simple. The answer is . . ." Lelaina fumbles through her notes, as though searching for a hearty summation, then shrugs. "The answer is, I don't know."

Lelaina is one of four friends disillusioned with the world and doubtful of the purpose of life, representing a generation that is "trying to find their own identity without any heroes or role models or anything," as she says later in the movie. The prevailing mood is most memorably captured by Troy, played by Ethan Hawke, who sits and broods and pontificates in between gigs with his band at a Houston coffee house. He answers the phone, "Hello, you've reached the winter of our discontent," and asserts that anyone who settles for easy answers is just "a pathological optimist." Reflecting on his parents' divorce and his father's cancer, Troy declares, "There's no point to any of this. It's just a random lottery of meaningless tragedy and a series of near escapes."

In moments, or months, of dark doubt, we are prone to agree with the four friends of *Reality Bites*, and reject the suggestion that there is any one true explanation of the meaning of our existence, or any grandiose purpose to our lives and our world. Politicians, preachers, and parents sometimes sound too self-satisfied as they give us their nice, neat packages of what they think life is all about and how we should make the world a better place. To some moviegoers, the malaise of *Reality Bites* is a viable alternative—a catatonic state of indifference to sacred questions. The only thing worse than wondering about the meaning of life is doubting that any such meaning is possible, or not caring that it is. This is fittingly called *nihilism*, from the Latin word *nihil* ("nothing").

This dour suspicion of ultimate purpose has worked its way into popular culture. At the end of an episode of the *The Simpsons*—which satirizes cutesy family sitcoms with their tidy resolutions and heavy-handed messages—the family gathers in the living room to ponder the events of the episode. Marge, the mother, struggles to sum everything up with a moral, but each one she comes up with is undermined by a contradicting detail. "Maybe there is no moral," Bart finally says. "Exactly," his father, Homer, concurs. "It's just a bunch of stuff that happened."

We sometimes agree when we look at life and its big questions. In a consumer society, in which contemplation is chased away by the urgency of the next purchase and the thrill of immediacy, it is hard to suppose that there is a *metanarrative* to life— a big-picture story of the history and future of the universe and our place in it. We have what Gordon Smith, in *Calling and Courage*, calls a "crisis of meaning." This crisis, he says, has us "perplexed about the meaning of who we are." After all, without a big picture in mind, the triviality of the little things in our lives can eat away our souls and our selves. The feeling that the world is meaningless soon translates into a feeling that our individual lives are meaningless, as it did for the author of the Book of Ecclesiastes:

"Meaningless! Meaningless! . . .
    Everything is meaningless!"

> What does [anyone] gain from all his labor
>   at which he toils under the sun? (Eccl. 1)

So our crisis of meaning is not just an intellectual, meta-physical puzzle. It sucks the oxygen out of every area of our lives. Without meaning, we fly around frantically and aimlessly. Smith says our crisis of meaning is in part a "crisis of hectic, unfocused activity" and of "overworked and confused lives." Too many people work hard in order to get ahead and pay the bills—but for little other reason. As we work longer hours and spend more time traveling to, from, or for our jobs, work begins to overwhelm our lives, even though for many people work is where they feel least spiritually alive, least whole, and most like they are just going through life's motions. The toll of all this work and all this rushing is a weary emptiness that saps our spirit and our sense of hope. With less time to interact, to walk, to read, and to reflect, we are disoriented, and we despair of orientation.

What passes for higher scholarship fuels our distrust of ultimate meaning. The emergence of postmodernism has dismantled a presumption of certainty with which people once lived. Postmodernism asserts that there is no absolute truth, no singular overall purpose to life, and that what humans perceive and believe is arbitrary and inapplicable to others. As suggested by the word *postmodernism*, this way of thinking is a response to the arrogant optimism of modernism, which believed that science and industry would lead humanity to a promised land of perfection. But what has replaced this naive faith is what *New York Times* critic A. O. Scott calls "a coy, postmodern suspicion of certainty."

Steven Garber, in *Fabric of Faithfulness*, says our quandary boils down to one question: "Why do you get up in the morning?" This question, he says, "gets at the relationship between what one believes about the world and how one lives in the world."

His question aligns with mine in this book: What is the meaning of life, and where are we going?

When we look in popular culture, in our work, and in higher education, the answers are often elusive. The meaning of life? "Who cares?" retorts popular entertainment. "Lose yourself in this ephemeral, momentary distraction." "Who has time?" retorts the working world, with its demands that we slave away for long hours and put aside questions of fulfillment and contemplation. "Lose yourself in the myriad of things you have to do. Go after that promotion as though it's all that matters." "Who can know?" retort our centers of higher learning. "Assumptions of truth and systems of belief are desperate delusions and means of control."

The result is a withering of the human spirit, the living spiritual death we see in the youth of *Reality Bites* and their lives of apathy and detachment. With these obstacles to a sense of meaning, who can live a life of spiritual vitality, continual refreshment, and broader purpose? Who has hope? Who can dream of heaven?

The road out of nihilism begins with cynicism about cynicism itself—the realization that nihilism and cynicism are themselves subjective, themselves "truth claims," themselves selections made by people who want to believe in something. "We are not made for monotony," writes Richard Winter in *Still Bored in a Culture of Entertainment*, nor should we be "negated to numbness." In fact, nihilism is no more natural or sensible to human beings than its odious opposite—a smug optimism or giddiness that is oblivious to the pain and doubt of others and of oneself. The recovery of meaning and hope lies between these two extremes. Hope comes not from an ironclad, flawless belief system that one forces on others, but from the cautious formation of a system of belief that is coherent if not certain, sound if not always sure. This formation, fraught as it is with frustration, seldom goes unrewarded. It can bring continual moments of awakening and arouse hope for the coming of heaven.

Wake-up Call

Neo has awoken but remains in a living nightmare. He has just undergone a reverse brainwashing at the hands of his new mentor, Morpheus, who has told Neo that his whole life until now was a fiction, a computer-programmed reality devised by machines to hide his slavery to them. He awakens in Morpheus's ship and asks, "Why do my eyes hurt?" Morpheus responds, "Because you've never used them before."

Neo's spiritual awakening in *The Matrix* is analogous to what is supposed to happen to people who encounter the transforming truth of Christ and the promise of eternal heaven. They are supposed to have their world turned upside down and see new dimensions of reality. Instead, many Christians continue to live lives of complacency, small-mindedness, and self-interest. Many believers accept the lies of society, going along with the ruse that what matters most are your material acquisitions and your personal achievements, and flirting with the faddish nihilism that there is no ultimate purpose for the world and our experiences.

In this swirl of distortions in which we carry on with our daily lives, we need a blinding ray of truth and light. We, like Neo, and like the apostle Paul on the road to Damascus, need an awakening if we are going to transform the worldly order to which we are enslaved. We need to know what is really going on. "Given our tendency to see and hear what we want to see and hear while disregarding the rest," writes David Dark in *Every-*

day Apocalypse, "we need whatever we can get in the way of an awakening." We need an apocalyptic kind of truth.

The word *apocalyptic* is intimidating. We have come to hear it as a reference to bizarre predictions of events associated with the end of the world, or, more accurately, the destruction of the world. This meaning of "apocalyptic," however, is merely a wrong turn away from the word's original definition. The Greek root *apokalypsis* meant "revelation" or "unveiling." We should restore this word to currency in Christianity and to its true meaning of "epiphany" and "awakening"—an awakening to what is really true, to what has been true all along. We should also restore our understanding of the book originally known as *Apokalypsis Iōannou,* the Revelation of John.

With its graphic characters—the dragon, the four-headed beast, and the rest—Revelation is the only apocalyptic book in the New Testament, and the only one to be regularly neglected by most Christians, other than those who try to match certain verses to certain current events and predict the end of the world. Their easy explanations only distract us from the central theme of the book. Revelation has an even bolder message to send.

What Christians need is a re-reading, or maybe a first reading, of the consummate chapter of Revelation, chapter 21. We need a new look at this chapter which focuses on its overt parallels to Isaiah 60—the Old Testament vision of heaven—and on how it sews up the entire biblical narrative building up to it. I have found it best to read Revelation with an eye toward its broadest themes and the overall direction of the story, rather than puzzling over each detail and hunting for hidden meaning. And so this book is not a breakdown of specific symbols in Revelation and their possible referents; it is about the final picture Revelation 21 paints for us. I try to follow the principle articulated by Paul Erb, in a quote I jotted down on a three-by-five note card in high school and have kept ever since: "Eschatology is . . . concerned not so much with the last things as with Him who is the first and the last."

The reward of reading Revelation this way is the kind of soul-warping wake-up call Neo experienced in *The Matrix*. Reading Revelation in search of an epiphany, a big-picture brand of truth telling—rather than for a woeful prediction of the end of the world—is the route to living everyday life on this planet with a new sense of meaning, and fanning the flickers of longing in our souls for the coming of eternity. Reading it with an eye toward how it ties up all the Bible's loose ends—capping a story that started in Genesis and continued through the Israelites and Isaiah to the Gospels and Paul and beyond—we can see Revelation not as a confusing and negligible epilogue to an otherwise inviting biblical story but instead as a window to the meaning and future of cosmic history. Transcending the artificial meaning of materialism and the chaotic meaning of nihilism, the apostle John's apocalyptic vision of heaven can give our lives coherence by merging our present with our future, making it clear to us just where we are going.

The key to overcoming our fear of the apocalyptic book of Revelation may be the realization that Revelation does not offer a glimpse of a remote world as much as an awakening to the truth about this one. We don't need to know how exactly the end of the world will come about as much as we need a clue to how our present world is building toward that end. Carol Zaleski says as much when she writes, "What Christians hope for is not a pleasant dream but a complete awakening, compared to which our present existence will look like troubled sleep." C. S. Lewis puts it even better in "The Weight of Glory": "Spells are used for breaking enchantments as well as inducing them," he says.

"And you and I have need of the strongest spell that can be found to wake us from the evil enchantment of worldliness which has been laid upon us."

The meaning of life, which *Reality Bites* considers impossible and the materialism of the Magnificent Mile renders all but irrelevant, depends on our awakening to what is around us—our natural planet (chap. 3), what we have built on it (chaps. 4 and 5), and the Creator and people we know within it (chap. 6). Donald Murray writes that his fellow journalists need to go beyond "seeing the obvious" and, with "skepticism . . . balanced by innocence," become "capable of seeing what is new." The same might be said of all of us, especially as we read Revelation 21.

The awakening that awaits is wondrous, as it was for Madeline L'Engle, who writes in *The Irrational Season*:

> When I think of the incredible, incomprehensible sweep of creation above me, I have the strange reaction of being fully alive. Rather than feeling lost and unimportant and meaningless, set against galaxies which go beyond the reach of the furthest telescopes, I feel that my life has meaning. Perhaps I should feel insignificant, but instead I feel a soaring in my heart that the God who could create all this can still count the hairs on my head.

This sense of wonder is the beginning of hope, the hope for completion of creation, the hope for eternity. Each molecule in the world and each moment of our lives bears witness to their own ultimate fulfillment. Easing our grip on the material goods and work routines with which we anesthetize ourselves to the transcendent, rejecting the foolhardy idea that truth and meaning are entirely elusive, and reopening our eyes as we reopen the Book of Revelation, we may get a glimpse of heaven itself, and reach for its glory without relenting.

THEATER OF GLORY

Heaven on Earth

I love thunderstorms. When I'm indoors, at least. I love watching raindrops skydive. Each drop's harrying descent ends with a devastating splash on the sidewalk; every second brings thousands such explosions. I love the rhythm the rain taps on the grass, on the pavement, and on my window, an unending round of applause. As it rains harder, the patter of the water starts to sound like speech, a conversation I can't comprehend but can't stop listening to.

I love the complexion of the sky as it turns to lead and releases its cargo. It gets ashen and angry, and the chatter gets louder. The smashing of thunderclaps fills the sky and makes everyone in a five-mile radius flinch. Fog rolls low and smudges the outlines of familiar trees and buildings. At night, lightning turns everything to instant day, as though God were flicking a light switch on and off. The streets, sewers, and trees swell with their sudden current, their rivulets splitting as they collide with stones.

To me, thunderstorms seem like nature reasserting itself. We have all but shut nature out of our lives with our houses and malls and cars, which we sometimes call "climate controlled." We are most likely to hear the chirping of birds or gushing of water on a relaxation tape rather than firsthand. But when the thunder smacks our eardrums, it reminds us that we are still on God's turf. We can build roofs over our heads and blot out the sky with skyscrapers, but we must still write "weather permitting" on our invitations to outdoor events. We still witness natural rules and rhythms in the world—thunderstorms, sunsets, moonlight, flowers, tides—simply by living on planet earth. We can construct all the artificial environments we want, but we will never completely shut out nature. Maybe it is that reminder that keeps me glued to the window as it is washed by the rain.

In the first verse of Revelation 21, John sets the stage for eternity. "Then I saw a new heaven and a new earth, for the first heaven and the first earth had passed away." John's vision is the same as Isaiah's centuries earlier: "Behold, I will create new heavens and a new earth."

Immediately, an important piece of the heavenly puzzle is in place: eternal heaven will be on earth. A new earth. Heaven will be *terrestrial*. We will not be floating on clouds, but walking on *terra firma*—firm ground. We will live among grass and trees, fields and forests, mountains, canyons, and waterfalls. We will not hover in the air; we will keep our footing.

Where will this new earth be, and what will happen to the old one? John's terminology gives us clues. He uses the Greek word *kainos* to mean "new" in the phrase "new heaven and a new earth." He does not use the word *neos*, which means "new" as in "different" or "other." *Kainos* means "new" as in "renewed" or "restored."

John says *kainos*. What he means, writes Anthony Hoekema in *The Bible and the Future*, is "not the emergence of a cosmos totally other than the present one, but the creation of a universe which, though it has been gloriously renewed, stands in continuity with the present one." This vision squares with Paul's prophecy in Romans 8, which foresees that "creation itself will be liberated from its bondage to decay." There's not much point in liberating this creation if an entirely different one is coming along. Instead, the old one will be made *kainos*, renewed, for the rest of eternity.

But why does John say "the first earth had passed away" if in the same sentence he shows that it isn't going anywhere? The answer, Hoekema says, is suggested in 2 Peter. "The day of the Lord will come like a thief," Peter says in 2 Peter 3. "The heavens will disappear with a roar; the elements will be destroyed by fire, and the earth and everything in it will be laid bare."

The key statement here is "the earth and everything in it will be laid bare." I had to read Albert Wolters's analysis in the *Westminster Theological Journal* to make sense of this passage. His analysis gets technical, but it has huge implications.

Many translations of this verse in 2 Peter read "burned up" instead of "laid bare," in keeping with the verse's image of fiery destruction, but Wolters says the translation of "burned up" comes from less reliable sources. The original Greek verb for "will be laid bare," he says, is *heuriskō*, and biblical translators have always struggled with it.

The proper way to translate *heuriskō*, Wolters says, is "will be found." (The English word *heuristic* means "aiding discovery or investigation.") It's the same verb Peter uses four verses later, when he says, "Make every effort *to be found* spotless, blameless and at peace with him." So verse 10 would read, "the earth and everything in it will be found." But what does this mean, that the earth "will be found"?

Wolters says we can solve this puzzle by looking elsewhere in 2 Peter and elsewhere in the Bible. The third chapter of 2 Peter is full of Greek verbs that describe what Wolters calls "a state of intense heat, as when a person is 'burning' with fever, or a piece of metal is red hot." But Peter doesn't use any words in this chapter that mean "going up in flames," in Wolters's words. So there is a lot of burning and melting going on, but not utter annihilation. Wolters connects this passage to Malachi 3, which says that at "the day of his coming," God will "sit as a refiner and purifier of silver, he will purify the Levites and refine them like gold and silver. Then the LORD will have men who will bring offerings in righteousness." It seems likely, Wolters says, that Peter had Malachi's words on his mind when he wrote 2 Peter 3.

So there will be a lot of destruction when God makes a new earth out of this old one, but it won't be the kind of destruction that obliterates something to smithereens. As with metal in a white-hot furnace, all impurities, deformities, and corruptions of planet earth will meet their fiery demise. All that will remain is goodness. Notice that Peter sets up this passage in verses 5 and 6 by talking about the "destruction" of the flood that soaked the stranded Noah for forty days. Obviously the earth was not destroyed in the flood; it was wiped clean.

If God's fiery judgment, as Peter foresees it, is in fact more like a blacksmith's fire than an incinerator, then the rest of 2 Peter 3 starts to fall into place. In verse 14, Peter tells readers to "make every effort to *be found* spotless, blameless and at peace with him." There's *heuriskō* again, in "to be found." Earlier, 1 Peter 1 says, "These [trials] have come so that your faith—of greater worth than gold, which perishes even though refined by fire—*may be proved* genuine and may result in praise, glory and honor when Jesus Christ is revealed." "May be proved" is another instance of *heuriskō*.

What Peter is doing by saying "will be found" and alluding to a refiner's fire is using a physical process to explain a metaphysical mystery—the awesome purification of the entire universe, including planet earth. Somehow "the entire cosmos," Wolters says, "is to be refined . . . [and] emerge purified."

Heaven will be on earth, *this* earth. The ground we stand on in heaven will be the same soil we stand on now, though it's doubtful we'll recognize it when God is finished refining and purifying it. God will take the earth and the rest of the universe and will heat it up and wring it out and squeeze all the sin and death out of it, until only a spotless new creation remains. And as it was in Genesis 1, when "God created the heavens and the earth," earth will again be the focal point of human existence (and so I will write "new earth" from now on to signify the new cosmos as a whole). Larry Richards tells us why:

> The Bible tells us that God created the far-flung material universe, but his efforts focused on our planet. It was this planet that God molded into an environment for living things. It was here that life sprang into existence when God spoke. It was here he came to scoop up the dust into which he breathed the breath of life. It was to planet earth God came to walk with Adam and

Eve in the Garden. . . . That [new] earth will also be the center of the universe, just as our earth is the center of the old.

Right away, this rearranges the picture of heaven that we have been trained to imagine. Eternal heaven will not, as I always used to assume, be a never-never land far away. It will not be airy and detached. It will be on this planet. As Hoekema writes, we will not spend our days "flitting from cloud to cloud" but will spend them on the new earth, "enjoying its beauties, exploring its resources, and using its treasures to the glory of God."

So we need to do away with any literal picture of eternal life as an irrelevant existence in a remote place. The images of harps and wings may symbolically suggest the happiness of heavenly life, but they do not set the actual scene. Although heaven is currently separated from this world, this arrangement is temporary, and we must learn to distinguish between heaven now and heaven forever (more on this in chap. 6). On the new earth, heaven and earth will be knit together again, as they were in the beginning.

The Theater of His Glory

Why is there a new earth? Why doesn't God ship us all out to one big cloud and let us float around for eternity? Why spend eternity among grass and trees, in human bodies, walking on soil and grass? Scripture gives strong hints, as we will see in a moment. But so does nature itself.

Nature has a rhythm all its own. We often ignore it. We live our lives surrounded by clocks, on our walls, on our wrists, on our desks, on the dashboards of our cars. It's easy to forget that the turning globe is the original clock, the ultimate way of marking the passage of time and measuring growth. In *A Sideways Look at Time*, Jay Griffiths reminds us of nature's temporal patterns, which she witnessed as never before in the forests of northern Thailand.

> The forest over the course of a day supplied a symphony of time, provided you knew the score. The morning held simplicity in its damp air, unlike the evening's denser wet when steam and smoke thickened the air. Backlit by sun, a huge waxy banana leaf at noon became green-gold stained glass. . . . Birds sang differently at different hours and . . . the whole orchestra of the forest altered, shifting with the sun's day.

Griffiths adds that some tribes we would consider primitive name the months for things in nature. They have the Deer month, the Strawberries month, the Mulberry month, the Bison month, the Bear month, the Chestnut month, and so on (while the rest of the world, including Christians, continues to name the months after pagan gods). There is a difference, says Griffiths, quoting author Jean Chesneaux, between "our wound-up time" and "the slow time of nature."

As Griffiths suggests, there is a cosmic rightness to creation, a timelessness that seems to sing its own song and weave its own mosaic. The vastness, the beauty, and the intricacy of nature make it a glorious work of art. G. K. Chesterton called nature "a symphony that plays on whether or not I stop to listen." In fact, the Greek word *kosmos*, for "created order," can be translated as "beautiful arrangement."

Why would this ever stop? Why bring this to an end? Why submit this labored-over masterpiece to a fiery demise rather than a dazzling rebirth?

The beauty and order of nature are not gratuitous. The tapestry does not exist for its own sake, just to be admired. Its grit and grandeur has a purpose. The prettiness has a point. Nature is, as Psalm 19 says in the King James Version, God's "handiwork." It has God's fingerprints all over it. John Calvin called creation "the theater of God's glory." It is a place where, and a way that, God performs.

And so creation isn't just a place for us to live or see beauty— it is a way to know God. Theologians use the Latin phrase *revelatio naturalis*—the revelation of nature. The Bible is one window to the mind of God; nature is another. Nature is not just there for us to take pictures of it; it is there to show us something. As Gerhard von Rad writes, "Creation not only exists, it discharges truth." It teaches, it illustrates, it suggests, it hints. I've always loved this line from Anne Lamott: "God is implicit in creation." Creation implies its Creator.

The Bible backs this up. "Since the creation of the world God's invisible qualities—his eternal power and divine nature— have been clearly seen, being understood from what has been made," Paul writes in Romans 1. As Wolters points out in *Creation Regained*, the phrase "what has been made" was written in Greek as "the works of the craftsman's art." That metaphor is apt. You cannot truly know the craftsman until you watch him at work at his craft, nor the painter until you see her paint. "He does beautiful work, doesn't he?" the cartoon character Ziggy says to a companion while taking in a glorious sunset. (Even in New Age and generic secular terminology, the name Mother Nature reflects our sense that creation has a person or personality—a creative and supervisory figure—behind it.) So trying to know God without knowing nature is as useless as writing a biography of Leonardo da Vinci without ever having seen the Mona Lisa.

God made the earth, informs us through it, and uses it as a vehicle of his presence, the theater of his glory. To deprive God of the earth for all eternity—which is what we do with our notions of heaven in the clouds—is to deprive the painter of his canvas. Sure, God could paint on something else, but why bother?

Our failure to see nature as God's craftsmanship is persistent. We forget whose ground we are standing on. Missionary John G. Paton once suggested to a native tribe that they dig a well. He drew curious looks. "They said water always came down from heaven, not up through the earth," Henry Emerson Fosdick recalls. Paton patiently explained that if they were to dig a well, "heaven could give them water through their own land." Why is it that we are always looking for God up in the skies, rather than in the streams at our feet?

The first verse of Revelation 21 addresses the questions I raised in the first two chapters. We should not fear or ignore heaven (chap. 1), since it does not mean the end of the world but a new beginning. In fact, we could take an advertisement for a PBS documentary on the origins of the universe as our new slogan to scrawl on apocalyptic signs: "The Beginning Is Near." And we should not be mystified about the meaning of life (chap. 2). We exist on this earth in order to get to know God through it and to anticipate the earth's eventual purification, its restored perfection.

To do this, we must do what the title of this book suggests: we must bring heaven down to earth. We must take our vague and distant pictures of a heaven in the clouds and make them less pie in the sky. We must make them more earthly. We must put some grass and trees—and soil and snow—in them. This does not mean we should make heaven more ordinary; there will be nothing ho-hum about the glistening planet that will emerge from the kind of fiery purification 2 Peter 3 foresees. But our conceptions of heaven must be more grounded, more concerned with the natural planet, as the Bible is. Paton had to tell that tribe with their heads in the clouds to look for heaven at their feet. Without losing any of our awe, we need to do the same thing.

Heaven will be on earth, *this* earth. Heaven will have what Griffiths saw in Thailand—the damp air of the morning, the waxy banana leaf turned green-gold by the sun, "the whole orchestra of the forest." Heaven will have the strawberry and the mulberry, the bear and the bison. It will have these things because they are among God's greatest hits, masterpieces in which we see him, books in which we can read him, a theater in which we can watch him perform. Heaven will have these things because God looks at them, at nature, and says, "It is good." When he says this on the new earth, it will be a joyous echo of the first time he said it, in the first chapter of Genesis.

We don't know just how God created the world, but we do know it was God who did it. "In the beginning God created the heavens and the earth," the first verse of the Bible says. God set the world, and human history, in motion. God created the world, conceived it from his infinite mind.

Christians disagree vehemently on how exactly this happened. Did God get all done with creation in the span of one week on the calendar? Or does Genesis poetically describe a process that happened much more gradually? Scripture seems to be deliberately vague on the particulars. In any case, the point is not the *when* of creation but rather the magnificence of the *what* and *why*: God created the universe, and he created it for the sake of goodness.

My favorite account of creation is not in Genesis but in Vassar Miller's poem "Morning Person":

God, best at making in the morning, tossed
stars and planets, singing and dancing, rolled
Saturn's rings spinning and humming, twirled the earth
so hard it coughed and spat the moon up, brilliant
bubble floating around it for good, stretched holy
hands till birds in nervous sparks flew forth from
them and beasts—lizards, big and little, apes,
lions, elephants, dogs and cats cavorting,
tumbling over themselves, dizzy with joy when
God made us in the morning too, both man
and woman, leaving Adam no time for
sleep so nimbly was Eve bouncing out of
his side till as night came everything and
everybody, growing tired, declined, sat
down in one soft descended Hallelujah

What God made, and how God made it, Miller suggests, was a delight. It was truly good. Seven times in Genesis 1, God proclaimed that creation was "good." This goodness turns out to be the purpose of all existence. Creation exists—we exist—to fulfill God's desire to embellish goodness. God didn't want creation to be *nice*—nice to look at, full of nice things. He wanted it to be *good*, full of fulfilling relationships and nurturing interdependencies.

This cosmic sense of rightness and wholeness is known in Hebrew as *shalom*. This wholeness, this compounded perfection, is "the webbing together of God, humans, and all creation in justice, fulfillment in delight," says Cornelius Plantinga. "Shalom, in other words, is the way things ought to be." The only question was whether the way things ought to be would be the way they would stay.

God formed the natural universe, suspended the stars, planted the grass, filled the lakes, stocked the fields with animals. And then he made humans. Humans were created to be unique among everything that was made, imbued with God's own image, lesser beings than him but still special beings of his, distinguished by their resemblance to their Creator.

And then God gave humans, and only humans, a choice. A crucial choice. Preserve the created order, by relishing and remaining in their posts as God's delegates and overseers of the fields and flocks, or disrupt the created order by coveting an impossible promotion to god-like status. Tragically, humans sought the impossible promotion.

When the serpent showed up in the Garden of Eden, he didn't want humans to switch allegiances from God to him, as you might expect. He wanted them to switch allegiances from God to themselves. He gave them the grotesque dream of supplanting God, of turning the tables and thus toppling the way things are supposed to be.

This dream of the impossible promotion remains with us today. It is the dream of everyone who has ever been self-centered. William Willimon writes in *Sighing for Eden* that this dream "pridefully denies one's proper, harmonious goodness; disfigures the orderly beauty of creation; destroys harmony; and introduces chaos." The dream of the divine self seems liberating, but it is terrifying, bringing not the heaven of omnipotence but instead what Tony Hendra calls the hell of "only your own self to hope in, only your own self to love . . . a prison with no door." The dream turns out to be a nightmare, and what has happened ever since Adam and Eve is that this nightmare has come true.

Last year in the Darfur region of Sudan, Janjaweed thugs attacked the villagers in Ab-Layha like beasts. Zahra Abdel Karim, a thirty-year-old woman, described the experience to a reporter for the *New York Times*. When the Janjaweed came, Karim said, they shot her husband, her seven-year-old son, and three of her brothers. They seized her four-year-old son from her arms and slashed his throat. Then they took Zahra and her two sisters away and gang-raped them. They slashed her leg with a sword and released her. She hobbled away, naked and bleeding.

At its root, the word *violence* relates to "violate." And "violate" means to cause something that shouldn't be. This nuance is often lost when we hear the word over and over in news reports. To us, violence means the use of weapons and the resulting destruction of places and people. Its numbing regularity gives us the illusion that violence is one of the natural rhythms of the world.

But it is not. It is the opposite—violence and sin are awful, agonizing, bloody, evil interruptions and perversions of the natural rhythms of the world. Sin, says Plantinga, is "the culpable disturbance of *shalom*," the interference with the way things are supposed to be. Sin makes a mess of what was made to be right and good. Sin can only be understood in terms of what it distorts and destroys: *shalom*.

We often forget this. Because goodness and order are still somewhat visible on the planet—more in some places than others—it is possible to delude ourselves, at least once in a while, into thinking that sin does not exist, or that it is only sporadic, or that it is only in Sudan and such places, or that it is only self-inflicted, or that it is mostly a minor matter of personal peccadilloes. Such illusions are our coping mechanisms in a world gone wrong. But they are lies. They numb us to the reality of the coming of the new earth.

What we need instead is a holy awareness—what psychologists call *cognitive dissonance*—of the fact that we are living in a world that is in many ways *wrong*, a world that is different from what was intended, what was established. The results of the sin that started when humans invited disorder into the world—the pain and injustice that we see around us—are not just too bad, they are wrong. They shouldn't be.

Every sinful thought, word, and action—from an unacted-upon adulterous fantasy to the murder of Zahra Abdel Karim's four-year-old son in Sudan—is a unique violation of a world created to lack that thought, word, or action. For those of us fortunate enough to never have experienced what Zahra did—witnessing the slaughter of her family, having her body intruded upon by thugs—it is easier to assume that things are basically right with the world and to take comfort in the thought that things would be all right if only a few bad people and their bad deeds could be removed. In this state of naïveté, we forget that the rightness of the world has been ruined—not completely wrecked but badly tangled. Often, when we hear of a distant war, an innocent prisoner, or a relative's cancer, we say, "How awful." What we should say instead is, "How wrong." Maybe that would help shatter our illusions and instill in us a holy restlessness for the recovery of the way things ought to be.

The tow truck driver in the movie *Grand Canyon*, more than most of us, lives with this fundamental awareness, as Plantinga notes. When the driver, played by Danny Glover, is stopped by a street gang while trying to help a man whose car has broken down, Glover doesn't protest that the gang's interference is arrogant or aggressive, although it is. Instead, he looks them in the eye and tells them that their behavior is a violation of order. "Man, the world ain't supposed to work like this," Glover says. "Everything's supposed to be different than what it is here."

He is right. And he is wise. This wrongness of the disruption of *shalom* is so important that Plantinga made it the title of his book about sin: *Not the Way It's Supposed to Be.*

I like how David Gushee articulates what Glover was getting at in *Grand Canyon.* "A proper biblical understanding of sin identifies it not just with particular acts or our propensity to do wrong but with a broader degradation of the human condition," Gushee writes. "Sin is not just a violation of God's moral order but also the disordered state of the human heart, human relationships, and human society. This disorder is the context in which we all live." We live in a constant state of compound decay. Creation isn't marred here and there by distinct sinful acts; it is polluted, poisoned, and pervaded by the stain of sin.

Sin spreads like grease on a napkin. Sin oozes, it creeps, it seeps. It functions as a virus. Wrongness embellishes wrongness; a minor lie breeds a major lie, an abusive father rears children who become abusive parents, a flirtatious joke becomes an adulterous affair. "Sin feeds on itself, has a life of its own once it is unleashed," Willimon writes. "Our sin infects our children, their children, the whole world."

Such a widespread, pervasive infection may seem cause enough for God to give up on his grand experiment of goodness. Like a perfect painting on which someone smears black streaks of ink, the original intention of *shalom*, of wholeness, of rightness, now seems remote and irretrievable. Would you fault God for casting aside his smock and paintbrush at the sight of such seeming ruination? Why not give up on the earth and opt for the heaven we always imagine—a flock of souls perched on the clouds, removed from the earth and from all memory of what was supposed to be? Why not call the creation project a failure, salvage the saints, and let it disappear? Would you blame

God, when his creatures threw his creation back in his face, for pitching it down the garbage disposal?

The marvel of the new earth, promised in Isaiah and 2 Peter and Revelation, is this: God is not giving up. The heavens and earth, soiled as they have been by sin, are not a failure, not a wreck, not irretrievable. The *shalom*—the heavenly wholeness, the right alignment of everything—is not beyond recovery. God, it turns out, has a holy stubbornness, a refusal to accept ruin. "If God would have to annihilate the present cosmos, Satan would have won a great victory," Hoekema observes. "For then Satan would have succeeded in so devastatingly corrupting the present cosmos and the present earth that God could do nothing with it but to blot it totally out of existence. But Satan did not win such a victory." *Shalom* is not out of God's reach.

Christianity is the only religion in which God reaches down to human beings and stoops to our level. Other religions worship a god whom humans must continually try to please, try to impress, try to elevate themselves to earn his favor and approach his level. God is the only god in all of human religion who lowers himself, as a way of exalting himself.

It is ironic, but it is no coincidence. *Shalom*, the order of creation, collapsed in Eden when humans wanted the impossible promotion: to become gods. *Shalom's* repair is achieved by reversing the process, with the improbable demotion when God becomes human. God tried throughout the Old Testament to make himself approachable, through rituals and sacrifices and covenants with the Israelites. But humans couldn't hold their end of the bargain. So God stooped down, became a man, and was butchered. That act atoned for the injustice of Eden and the subsequent sin and suffering in the world.

We always assume that Jesus Christ died on the cross to save people's souls. But the Bible does not limit the purpose of the cross this way; it extends it to creation. Romans 8 says "that the creation itself will be liberated from its bondage to decay and brought into the glorious freedom of the children of God." Nature itself will be free from sin. Not just souls, but also soil. Not just people, but the theater in which God performs for them and reveals himself to them.

Even without this biblical promise, it makes sense to guess that heaven would end up on this earth. It fits. It gives history a sense of completion. The continuity of the story—earth created, ruined, and restored—is utterly logical and utterly consistent with God's character. It isn't clear from the Bible why God would—as I used to think—rescue individual people to exist in a remote spiritual state for eternity, but consider the rest of what he made irrelevant and let it fall away. In this view, the earth would be like a bad memory, intolerable and eagerly dismissed.

But the biblical story suggests the ending we find in Revelation 21. God created the earth, watched its perversion, intervened and introduced its restoration, and will complete its restoration with its purification and perfection. "Earth," Richards says, "is the center of the universe simply because the grand drama of sin and salvation has been acted out on its stage." So it is fitting that eternal heaven will happen here.

Many popular prophecies ignore or deny this continuity. They suggest that our ultimate destiny is to escape the earth, to fly toward the sky, never to return. They hear biblical warnings about the end of sin and the closing of the book of the current age, and they assume the warnings apply to everything in the universe, not just sin. But this distorts the central biblical message. This message is that heaven will not be an *escape* from this earth but a *renewal* of this earth. Heaven will be a relevant resolution of the story of creation. Sin and its patterns of perversion will be bleached out of the original creation once and for all. *Shalom* will again flourish on the earth.

The purpose of heaven is not to make us happy but to make things right, to win back *shalom* and usher in the return of rightness and wholeness. Once again, God, creation, creatures, and their mutually nourishing relationships will combine to form such a delightful conglomeration that they will, as Plantinga puts it enticingly, "keep building like waves of a passion that is never spent."

Bondage to Decay

In the meantime, the earth groans. The rupture of *shalom*, and the wait for its restoration, is taking its toll on the earth—not just on human beings but the physical planet. "The whole creation has been groaning as in the pains of childbirth," Paul says in Romans 8. The groans will not subside until "creation itself will be liberated from its bondage to decay."

Those groans can be seen and heard in nature around us, as *Time* described in a cover story on global warming.

> Glaciers, including the legendary snows of Kilimanjaro, are disappearing from mountaintops around the globe. Coral reefs are dying off as the seas get too warm for comfort. Drought is the norm in parts of Asia and Africa. El Niño events, which trigger devastating weather in the eastern Pacific, are more frequent. The Arctic permafrost is starting to melt. Lakes and rivers in colder climates are freezing later and thawing earlier each year. Plants and animals are shifting their ranges poleward and to higher altitudes, and migration patterns for animals as

diverse as polar bears, butterflies and beluga whales are being disrupted.

Human beings bear some responsibility for this. We were entrusted, in Genesis 1, with the stewardship of the earth. Instead, human beings turned the earth into something to conquer and plunder, disrupting its rhythms and wasting its resources. We have lost sight of the earth as God's sanctuary. Today, "land is pure commodity to be bought and sold without regard to the deep connections of land and occupant," writes Walter Brueggemann. "At the present time, the tilt in public posture and policy is all toward economics at the expense of the environment."

Because humans were charged to care for the earth, humans are responsible for the current mess that it is in. But we are also meant to be part of the solution. God will one day restore the earth and make it a new earth, and is already working to undo nature's "bondage to decay." And so we should be too. "The human creature is called to work with God . . . both with and on behalf of the rest of creation," writes William Dyrness before introducing this intriguing idea: "For it is only in relation to God's presence and work in creation that the creature finds its meaning."

Our duty is to help heal the natural creation, in anticipation of its final, glorious rebirth. We are to keep our charge as responsible managers, as stewards, and strive to live in a way that refrains from extending humanity's abuse of nature and instead looks for ways to reverse it. This may sound grandiose and idealistic, but as Garret Keizer writes in the *Christian Century*, "The devil has two horns: the horn of pride that says there is nothing we *ought* to do, and the horn of despair that says there is nothing we *can* do."

Some Christians scorn environmentalists for their excesses and their methods, and sometimes with good cause. The political rhetoric of some environmentalists can be hostile and risks worshiping creation instead of the Creator. Keizer warns of environmental "idolatry" and warns of "making environmentalism into an identity," which happens when "the little group to which I belong becomes my sole basis for self-understanding and the farthest boundary of my love."

Environmentalists also tend to be eschatologically numb, with no sense of the big picture, of an earth destined for eternal purification by God. Instead, many concern themselves with minimal gains and goals and remain blind to the widespread, deep-seated human folly that led to the abuse of the earth in the first place. As surely as land-hungry and material-greedy human beings plundered the earth before, humans will do it again. Keizer wisely asks, "What good would it do to clean up the whole earth tomorrow, only to foul it up the day after?"

But say this for environmentalists, however disagreeable you may find their methods: they have the awe-for-creation part right. They have a sense of the sacredness of our natural surroundings and a sense of shame in the fouling of those surroundings. They have a sense of wonder at creation, even if their wonder seldom extends to the Creator—as though they are delighting in a delicious meal without giving a thought to the cook.

To be consistent with the message of the new earth given in the first verse of Revelation 21, Christians must recover awe for creation and be fervent in our efforts to be stewards of it and prevent its further injury. We need to see the earth not just as a keepsake worth protecting but as God-trod territory worth our wonder. "The issues to be faced cannot be dealt with by ideological sloganeering," says Brueggemann. "What is required, rather, is a reengagement with *environment as creation.*"

Scott Hoezee puts this idea in provocative terms in *Remember Creation*. He speaks of the renewal of creation as something the devil detests.

> What God loves, the devil hates. . . . Given that the Son of God died to redeem the entire universe from its bondage to decay, is it any surprise that the devil even now seeks to undermine and sully the created splendors of this world? Given that one day soon God will renew everything from primroses to quasars, is it any surprise that the devil is furiously seeking to block that re-creation?

What the devil seeks to block, we must advance.

The future of the earth determines how we view the present earth, and how we respond to urgent environmental crises. If we believe what is portrayed in popular prophecy—that earth is destined to perish and that humans will flee to a remote state of spiritual bliss with God—then current environmental problems are of minimal concern. If earth is going to perish anyway, what is the big deal about pollution? If anything, pollution is only speeding up the inevitable and bringing us closer to the return of Christ. This escapist brand of Christianity turns faith into a get-out-of-earth-free card.

To people who believe this interpretation of biblical prophecy, environmental issues are a lost cause. To such Christians, the importance of driving cars that do not waste fuel and protecting wildlife reserves is remote. To them, environmentalism will seem like an especially foolish idea. They would not be the least bit amused to get a flyer on their windshield that resembles a parking ticket, like the one I once found on the sidewalk. Intended for sport utility vehicles and other gas-guzzling cars, the fake ticket read, "This form of transport incurs costs . . . which have not been included in the retail price. Your operation of this vehicle makes you personally liable for the following: . . . depletion of non-renewable resources, smog-related health problems, climate change."

To Christians who read the words of 2 Peter 3 and Revelation 21, however, and hear the prophecy of the coming of a new earth—a renewed earth, a purified earth, this same earth after a spell in the refiner's fire—stewardship of the current planet is a matter of hearing and obeying the biblical message. It is a call to action, a call to responsible living, careful use of natural resources, minimal production of waste. The authors of *Redeeming Creation* call for the church to shape a new generation of stewards who are "biblically informed, morally responsible and passionately devoted," conscious of and committed to their duty to care for the earth. "It is their voices and their lives that will shape the future of ethics, policy and management of God's creation."

Caring for the earth now is an act of witness to the coming of the new earth, when creation's groans are ended and nature again flourishes to the glory of God. Caring for the earth now shows that we expect this to happen. We are stewards now because we expect to continue in the role for eternity, responsibly managing the natural world. This is why Keizer sees nature "both as an objective, biological reality, and as a vivid interior hope."

The Bible enforces this hope in the one place it talks about the rapture, the time when believers are seized into the clouds to meet the returning Christ. "The Lord himself will come down from heaven, with a loud command, with the voice of the archangel and with the trumpet call of God, and the dead in Christ will rise first," Paul writes in 1 Thessalonians 4. "After that, we who are still alive and are left will be caught up together with them in the clouds to meet the Lord in the air."

The Greek word for "meet" here, *apantēsin,* is rarely used in the New Testament, but when it is, it means to receive and escort a dignitary. This is the same word used in Matthew 25: "At that time the kingdom of heaven will be like ten virgins who took their lamps and went out to *meet* the bridegroom." The women waiting outside the wedding banquet intended to go and greet the bridegroom when he arrived and escort him inside. The other instance of *apantēsin* in the Bible is similar. In Acts 28, Luke writes that he and Paul were invited by some brothers to stay with them. "The brothers there had heard that we were coming, and they traveled as far as the Forum of Appius and the Three Taverns to *meet* us." Then they all traveled to the initial destination together.

In the same way, Paul suggests, we will be caught up into the air to meet the Lord and escort him as he returns to earth, his destination. The common portrayal of the rapture, in which saints are scooped up off the earth never to return, blatantly ignores the meaning of *apantēsin;* it suggests saints will keep on going all the way into the skies and never look back. But *apantēsin* does not mean meeting and leaving; it means meeting and escorting, the way the virgins planned to escort the bridegroom into the wedding banquet and the believers escorted Paul and Luke back to their home. *Apantēsin* means picking someone up at the airport; it doesn't mean getting on a plane and taking off. Paul is saying that we will rise to welcome Christ and escort him back to earth.

So the question is, What kind of earth will we escort Christ back to? How are we preparing for his arrival, when we form his welcoming party? Will we bring him back to an earth that we have abused and neglected? Will we show him a place that we have made a mess of while we called it our home? Will it seem that we didn't give much thought to the state of our natural surroundings and thought only about our inner spiritual lives? Or will we escort Christ back to an earth that we clearly treasured, that we cared for and managed as responsibly as we could, for his glory? Will it look like we were getting ready for him to come back?

"This planet is more than just a stopover on your way to heaven," says Michael Wittmer in *Heaven Is a Place on Earth*. "It is your final destination." No matter what popular prophecy says, we are preparing the earth for eternity, not idling here before we leave. We're not waiting to depart; we've arrived. We must not make the mistake of the tribe Paton told to dig a well, the tribe that was bewildered because they were looking for water from the skies and ignoring the heaven at their feet. Instead, we must actively anticipate the final removal of the curse of sin by working now, in our small and flawed ways, for the restoration of creation. We must show the world that we are expecting what Revelation says: that heaven will come down to earth forever. God is not giving up on the planet. Neither should we.

BEATING OUR SWORDS

The Greatest Commission

I f your pictures of heaven are anything like mine were when I was growing up, they're rather empty. Whether you picture heaven in a meadow or the middle of the air, the scene is probably serene but also vacant. Not much happens. Heaven is peaceful but rather blank.

The news that heaven will be on a new earth helps fill this void. As in the Garden of Eden, heaven will have trees with leaves and fruit, fields of flowers, and riverbanks caressed by waters. It's paradise. But it's still a little quiet. Trees and leaves help, but they may suggest that heaven will be like a Buddhist monastery, where we sit still and silent and soak in the harmony with nature. Heaven is a nice existence, but it seems like an idle existence.

Huckleberry Finn thought so. In Mark Twain's classic novel, Huck's teacher tries to impress upon him that good behavior will be rewarded in heaven. "She went on and told me all about the good·place. She said all a body would have to do there was to go around all day long with a harp and sing, forever and ever. So I didn't think much of it." Michael Wittmer comments, "Huckleberry Finn is right: Heaven does sound boring."

The Garden of Eden, however, was at the beginning of the Bible, and eternal heaven is at the end. And as pleasant as our peaceful pictures of paradise are—and as surely as they capture an important aspect of the afterlife—they don't measure up to the kind of heaven promised by biblical prophecy.

In the second verse of Revelation 21, John sees "the Holy City, the new Jerusalem" coming down to earth to be God's eternal dwelling. Not a garden, but a busy, bustling city. Isaiah sees the same thing in his prophecy, in Isaiah 60. As Richard Mouw points out in his intriguing study of Isaiah's heavenly vision, *When the Kings Come Marching In*, Isaiah's strikingly detailed account makes heaven sound like a busy place. There is a lot going on, with much to see and hear and do.

In fact, Isaiah's vision of the heavenly city seems less like a prophecy than an *inventory*. There is a lot coming into the city, and Isaiah, in chapter 60, seems to want to get it all down.

> Herds of camels will cover your land,
>   young camels of Midian and Ephah.
> And all from Sheba will come,
>   bearing gold and incense
>   and proclaiming the praise of the LORD.

All Kedar's flocks will be gathered to you,
the rams of Nebaioth will serve you;
they will be accepted as offerings on my altar,
and I will adorn my glorious temple.
Who are these that fly along like clouds,
like doves to their nests?
Surely the islands look to me;
in the lead are the ships of Tarshish,
bringing your sons from afar,
with their silver and gold,
to the honor of the LORD your God. . . .
[All will] bring you the wealth of the nations—
their kings led in triumphal procession. . . .
The glory of Lebanon will come to you,
the pine, the fir and the cypress together,
to adorn the place of my sanctuary.

Ships, cedars, and camels. The wealth of the nations. Kings led in procession. Isaiah's heaven is not so much a meadow as a market. It's the New York Stock Exchange and a presidential inauguration rolled into one. There is money and pomp, power and pageantry.

This, Isaiah says, is heaven's opening ceremony. Heaven begins with a parade.

I remember looking forward to the local parade every Fourth of July when I was growing up. My sister and I would take our places along the sidewalk and watch eagerly as the fire trucks, motorcycles, and politicians waving from uncovered cars passed by. Some threw candy toward the sidewalk, and we dove for it. We would plug our ears when the fire engines drove by and blasted their horns. My mouth gaped as I looked up the trucks' broad, bright red sides, awestruck by their size and strength.

Why all the fire trucks and politicians? At the time, I was too busy eating candy to wonder what it all meant. Now it's clearer to me; what the city does every Fourth of July is put its power and color on display, show it off, and ask us to bask in it. It's a way of saying, "This is what we are all about. Let's admire and celebrate our trucks, our leaders, and our name."

Isaiah 60 sees the greatest parade of all time at the unveiling of eternal heaven. This parade has trading ships and flocks of animals, kings and gold and silver. This is a parade you are going to want a good seat for. People will line up for miles to see all of this magnificent display as it passes by and enters into the heavenly city. But it's not just a good show; the spectacle of the kings and trading ships, like the politicians and fire trucks in a Fourth of July parade, has a purpose. They give glory. They honor and magnify the name of the one they are marching for. They march, Isaiah says, "to the honor of the LORD your God . . . to adorn the place of my sanctuary, [to] glorify the place of my feet." They decorate heaven, and in so doing, they worship.

What will happen when the parade is over? Will we finally get some peace and quiet? Probably—the parade doesn't mean that heaven will be a cacophonous frenzy. Still, there is plenty in the visions of Isaiah and John to suggest that the pageantry and spectacle of this parade—and the commerce and politics the parade celebrates—will last long after the parade is over. "The ships of Tarshish" Isaiah sees will keep on sailing and never stop.

To find out why, we must ask why the ships of Tarshish were built to begin with.

Commissioned to Cultivate

The Garden of Eden was an unfinished masterpiece. It was beautiful, and more importantly, as God said, it was "good." It was without flaw. But part of the reason God made human beings was to make it even better. Wittmer has a great line about this: "God," he says, "did not create a static world."

After God created humans, he gave them a mission, a purpose: "God blessed them and said to them," in Genesis 1, " 'Be fruitful and increase in number; fill the earth and subdue it. Rule over the fish of the sea and the birds of the air and over every living creature that moves on the ground.' " To "fill" means to reproduce, and to "subdue" means to rule over nature as God's subordinate managers. But there is much more to filling and subduing than that, as Mouw explains: "The earth was also to be 'filled' by the broader patterns of [humans'] interactions with nature and with each other. They would bring order to the Garden. They would introduce schemes for managing its affairs … [and] transform untamed nature into a social environment."

The filling and subduing began almost immediately. Mouw imagines the first time Adam and Eve broke off a branch and used it as a rake to clear and smooth their living space, and the first time they agreed to take turns raking each morning. Just like that, they had an instrument and an arrangement of responsibilities. Just like that, they had begun building upon the way creation was. They had designed a tool and designed a structure of duties for the purpose of bringing order and greater enjoyment to the Garden of Eden.

We have been filling the earth with our tools and our organizing ever since. Humans went on to make plows for digging into the earth and planting seeds in it, and vehicles to get around it faster, and buildings in which many people can live and work.

Humans design economies, agreeing how much a product or piece of currency will be worth or for what it can be exchanged. Humans set up businesses, organizing the sellers and the selling of many products. Humans establish governments, setting up a system by which a body of people have authority and keep social order. The U.S. Constitution, for example, is a design for a method of government. Humans make art, taking tools and colored materials and making works that render the world more vivid. Humans make families, reproducing and living together in intimate units. Humans make traditions—habits, beliefs, and practices that have value to groups of people, such as a Fourth of July parade.

Human beings do all of these things because we are following our mission, the reason we were made. We were made to fill the earth with our population, our products, and our ways of organizing ourselves. We do this out of instinct, obeying God's command to "fill the earth and subdue it."

What God was telling humans to do was to make *culture*. He created nature and then told us to add culture—not because he couldn't, but because he wanted to give us the freedom to produce and organize, and then revel with us in what we came up with. He wants us to use our dynamic energy to enhance creation. Because we are made in his image, we have the same instinct he has to make things. So that's what we've been doing ever since the Garden of Eden.

Our purpose—the meaning of our lives—is to make culture, to develop and form the world of nature. Ever since Adam and Eve broke off that tree branch, we have been cultivating the garden; in fact, the Latin word *cultura* means "cultivation." Some scholars call God's command in Genesis 1:28 the "cultural mandate"—a mandate to make culture. "Mandate" can sound like something we do only out of obligation, so perhaps a better phrase is "cultural commission." When a king or president commissions an artist to make a work of art, the ruler is saying to the artist, "Come up with something through your creative ability and enjoyment of your skill, and then give it to me to beautify my palace or public building." God says the same thing to humans: "Come up with something, out of duty and out of enjoyment. Make me some culture."

This sense of the word *culture* may sound a little strange at first. We often think of culture in terms of fine art, such as the paintings in an art museum. We may say, "I'm going to the opera to experience some culture." Or we may think of culture as the unfamiliar symbols and practices of other ethnic groups—exchange students, for example, live in other countries to experience other cultures. But these are specific meanings that have come from a general idea: culture is the stuff of which human life consists. I like Cornelius Plantinga's succinct definition: "Human culture is the sum of what humans produce and of the ways in which they are organized for life together."

Humans fill the earth with culture and subdue the earth with culture. The word *subdue* is a helpful one, once we see its roots. We understand "subdue" as "exercise authority over," "dominate," and even "make silent." A parent subdues a crying child; a king subdues a rebellion. However, the Latin word *subducere* meant "to draw from below"; it was used to describe the process of drawing water from a well.

This sense of the word *subdue* is a good description of what to do in response to God's command to be culture makers. We are to draw out from the earth a new beauty, a new reality, that lies beneath the surface and awaits our ability and skill to make it come to be. I've always loved this line from William Dyrness: "Culture is what we make of creation." We are born to embellish creation, to take its goodness and beauty and make it even more beautiful and good. Think of one of the classic lines from the movie *Casablanca*: "He's like any other man, only more so." We are to take creation and make it *more so*—a little more complex, a little more enjoyable, and a little better.

What we often do instead is fill the earth with a lot of junk. Because culture making is a human process, it is prone to the prideful patterns of human behavior introduced by sin. As we saw last chapter, sin ushered in the perversion of *shalom*, the way things are supposed to be. No longer does everything relate to each other and edify each other the way it was made to do. The same goes for culture. The things we produce and the ways we organize now display the disturbances and perversions of pride, greed, and corruption.

So the filling and subduing of the earth continues, but often to evil ends. We fill the earth with waste. We bring out the worst in it rather than the best in it. Instead of the beautiful subduing that is like drawing water, we practice the cruel subduing of violent oppression. We were made to give greater beauty to a beautiful creation, but instead we make a mess. Plantinga laments culture making gone awry:

> Great scientists use their excellent minds to dream up megade-structive intercontinental ballistic missiles. Filmmakers put a good face on divorce or godlessness. Some politicians try to become dictators, and some doctors get more interested in wealth than in healing. Some ministers preach sermons that are popular but not true. . . . Nations boast of their destructive might. . . . Racists pride themselves on their color. . . . The earth is full . . . of trash as well as treasure.

What whets our appetite for heaven is, once again, the profound awareness that this is not the way it's supposed to be. We try to tolerate the existence of evil in the world, to put up with the trash alongside the treasure, take the good with the bad. But we live a lie if we lose sight of the fact that *shalom* has been disrupted, that the right alignment of things has been bent of out shape. Scientists were not made to use their brains to make bombs; politicians were not meant to use their power to puff up their sense of self. Plowshares were not meant to be beaten into swords, turning growing fields into battlefields. The builders of the tower of Babel were not supposed to say, "Let us make a name for ourselves." The builders of the ships of Tarshish were not supposed to say the same thing. Culture was not supposed to be turned into bragging rights.

This twistedness is a result of the initial human choice to seek the impossible promotion. But today, it is the product of a hundred small choices we make every day. "Human culture is a symphony in which we can all play either well or poorly," writes Quentin Schultze. "We enter the stage of God's creation and make our music. When we play well, in tune with our gifts and God's score, the music is magnificent. We pour spiritual life into a luscious creation. . . . On the other hand, when we stubbornly write our own score, we orchestrate dissonance, destruction and despair."

The problem with the perversion of things often lies in the perverter. The materialism on Michigan Avenue in Chicago I described in chapter 2 comes from people's unhealthy relationships to things. The problem with materialism is not that materials exist but that we are not relating to them in a proper and beautiful way. There's nothing wrong with buying things and enjoying them; the problem is becoming so fixated on acquiring, owning, and having things that they cloud our vision. All these things on Michigan Avenue were made because humans are culture makers, following the cultural commission, but thing making and thing buying got out of hand.

Excessive thing making is especially prevalent in industrial societies, which run on the large-scale making and selling and buying of things. We have, as a professor of mine put it, an "industrial fascination with the conversion of matter." This has always been true in Chicago. More than a century before Michigan Avenue became a retail paradise, Chicago was the industrial capital of the world. Millions of hogs and stacks of wheat and pieces of lumber passed through Chicago's trading posts and factories in order to be processed and sold.

This industrial transformation of the city of Chicago was, in many ways, disastrous. Natural resources were used with reckless abandon, without regard to whether they could be replenished. Business owners were so greedy for more money that they commanded their industries to make as many things as possible, without regard to their waste. The city stunk; sewage and other garbage were poured into the Chicago River, and pollution from the factories literally cast a cloud over the city. William Cronon, in *Nature's Metropolis*, describes the scene he saw as a child riding into Chicago in the mid-twentieth century:

> The city announced itself to our noses before we ever saw it. . . . The place remains in my memory as a gray landscape with little vegetation, a clouded sky hovering over dark buildings, and an atmosphere that suddenly made breathing a conscious act. I remember especially one smokestack with dense rusty orange vapor rising like a solid column far into the sky before it dissipated. We always saw it there, every year, and it signaled our entrance into The City.

Is this any way to fill the earth? Is this any way to make culture? Is this a good attempt to cultivate the garden—to pursue profit in such a wasteful way that the city becomes unlivable and the natural landscape soiled?

Chicago's factories are mostly gone, but industrial dominance continues. The word *development* is an economic buzzword that illustrates the same gluttonous appetite for culture making. We speak of developed land as land that has been built upon in order to turn a profit—"condo developments," for example—and we think of an empty lot as "undeveloped" because it is not as profitable as land with buildings on it. The "fascination with the conversion of matter" that leads us to cultivate the garden with little regard to environmental and aesthetic beauty continues to cast a pall over our culture making.

Part of the problem with our industrial imperatives to produce and consume so carelessly is that we have reduced our concept of culture to its economic and political components. To us, the interaction of people and the making and selling of goods are just ways to make money and increase our wealth. We often encounter salespeople who have taken no interest in us as people, but see us only as customers off whom to make a profit—not people but "consumers," links in an economic process. How different would the world be if people were not so hell-bent on profit, but instead appreciated interaction with people and the use of goods for the sake of their inherent pleasure, and for God's sake?

The reduction of the idea of culture from its purpose to embellish creation to its function in obtaining money and power shows up in larger ways. Many social thinkers, for instance, study politics and economics merely as the transfer of power and money. Karl Marx famously stated that all industrial economic activity existed only as a way for the wealthy to oppress the poor. Historians often reduce history to the story of who won which wars and was king of how much territory at what time. The news media tend to cover elections not as a selection of policy makers, but as a game of power, with winners and losers of influence.

All these academics, economists, and journalists are interested in the balance of power and the wealth of nations, but they cannot explain why economics and politics exist. They cannot consider the process of culture making for its own sake, for God's sake. Ask most scholars of economics and politics and history why humans live cultural lives, and you will get either a blank stare or the default theory that humans make culture in order to survive. Dyrness says we all share their blind spots. "We have come to take for granted that the world must be understood, and therefore life must be lived, on its own terms. We no longer believe these things exist for God." And so we ignore the idea of heaven.

To get the idea of heaven back, we must ask the questions that are being neglected. Why do humans exist and experience cultural life? The answer is that God created us to cultivate the earth, to fill it and subdue it, not for our own prosperity but for his glory. We have lost sight of that purpose. Until we recover it, we have little chance to see where all this culture making is going.

Destructive Devotion

To see what becomes of our culture making, and how all of this trash is disposed, follow the ships of Tarshish as they sail right into Isaiah's vision in Isaiah 60.

In the days of Isaiah, the ships of Tarshish were magnificent trading vessels admired around the world. They carried riches around the Mediterranean Sea and brought wealth to their trading partners. King Solomon's fleet of ships that traded with Tarshish was among his prized possessions, 2 Chronicles 9 tells us: "Every three years [the fleet] returned, carrying gold, silver and ivory, and apes and baboons." You can imagine how the first hearers of Isaiah 60 remembered their eagerness as they raced to the ports to get a glimpse of the mighty ships from Tarshish—as eager as I was as I waited for the fire engines in the Fourth of July parade—and the awe they had for that armada.

Many archaeologists assume that Tarshish (named for Noah's great-great-grandson) was the ancient city of Tartessus, located near the Strait of Gibraltar in what is now southern Spain. This location at the mouth of the Mediterranean Sea was perfect for a port, and it made Tartessus a prosperous and powerful city; the right to trade with it was a feather in your cap. As Psalm 72 says, getting goods from Tarshish was a fine tribute to a king.

Isaiah's audience was awed not only by the wealth and size of the ships from Tarshish but also the distance they traveled. Tarshish probably marked the westernmost point of the known world. When Jonah sailed for Tarshish (before getting swallowed by a fish along the way), he was clearly hoping to get as far away from Israel as he possibly could (and from the Assyrian capital of Nineveh, the *easternmost* point of the known world). It was like going to the North Pole.

Because of their wealth, their mileage, and their might, the ships of Tarshish were among the most visible symbols of commercial power of their day. They were the ancient equivalent of the Coca-Cola corporation. Today the Coca-Cola logo is recognized all over the world. The Coca-Cola corporation earns billions of dollars each year and has thousands of workers and millions of customers. The sight of the logo makes us think of a mighty corporation, of commercial success, of a company's ability to participate in the daily lives of people. The same was true of the ships of Tarshish. They were emblems of human pride and profit.

But God is not impressed by the might of humans' commercial empires. Isaiah says this in his prophecy. In Isaiah 2 he announces:

> The LORD Almighty has a day in store
>   for all the proud and lofty,
>   for all that is exalted . . .
> for every ship of Tarshish
>   and every stately vessel.
> The arrogance of man will be brought low
>   and the pride of men humbled;
> the LORD alone will be exalted in that day.

These ships of Tarshish, these symbols of human might, wealth, and self-reliance, would be humiliated in the day of the Lord, and their humility would give glory to God, the only worthy recipient of glory.

The destruction of the ships of Tarshish and other commercial idols is a recurring theme throughout the Old Testament. "You destroyed them like ships of Tarshish, / shattered by an east wind," says Psalm 48. Jeremiah 10 tells us why: the wealth of Tarshish was used to build idols. "Hammered silver is brought from Tarshish, and gold from Uphaz. What the craftsman and goldsmith have made is then dressed in blue and purple." The next verse contains a rebuke: "But the LORD is the true God; he is the living God, the eternal King."

The strange thing is that after all this destruction of the ships of Tarshish, the ships show up in Isaiah's vision of the eternal heavenly city. "Surely the islands look to me; in the lead are the ships of Tarshish . . . with their silver and gold, to the honor of the LORD your God." How can the ships be destroyed and then brought into the city? Or will they be brought into the city and then destroyed? Or is the prophesied destruction an empty threat, before God changes his mind and leaves them alone?

One enticing explanation, Mouw says, is that the ships, like the earth in 2 Peter 3, will be purified, transformed in a fiery inferno that incinerates every trace of sin and pride. Here's how he explains his theory:

> We might think here of the "breaking" of the ships of Tarshish as more like the breaking of a horse rather than the breaking of a vase. The judgment here is meant to tame, not destroy. The ships of Tarshish will be harnessed for service in the Holy City. . . . It is not, then, the ships *as such* that will be destroyed; it is their former *function* that will perish.

This kind of transforming destruction—rather than anni-hilating destruction—is familiar in the Old Testament as well as in 2 Peter. In Deuteronomy 2, Moses reports that when God delivered an enemy king to Israel, "we took all his towns and completely destroyed them." But the Hebrew word for "destroyed" here does not mean ending the existence of some-thing; it means ending their idolatry and consecrating them to God. The word for "destroyed" here in Deuteronomy 2 is the same word that is translated as "devoted" in Joshua 6: "The city and all that is in it are to be devoted to the LORD. . . . All the silver and gold and the articles of bronze and iron are sacred to the LORD and must go into his treasury." When we read these passages, we are taken aback by the fact that such evil items are allowed in God's holy place. But God is glorified by their rededication to him. To God, the destruction of idolatrous wealth and the devotion of it to him go hand in hand.

So God is not appalled by the *existence* of the ships of Tarshish; he is appalled by the *pride* people take in the ships of Tarshish. And this is what he has to get rid of before heaven can come in all its glory. The hubris and bragging rights of human leaders and human empires must all be banished before *shalom* is recovered. But as sternly as these prideful patterns are condemned, the objects of pagan worship themselves still have a future as tools of service to God. Indeed, God's declaration in Revelation 21:5 is not, "I am making all new things," but, "I am making all things new!"

Those things include the ships of Tarshish, or equivalent commercial powers. In Isaiah's vision, the ships of Tarshish are back in business, only this time with a new owner and master. No longer will they bring honor to a distant seaport empire. No longer will the wealth and glory of the Coca-Cola corporation go to the company's CEO in Atlanta. This time, the means of human pride and wealth will glorify God. Idols will be destructively devoted.

The same holds for culture in general. God will devote, not destroy, the culture we have made that has gone awry—the things and the ways we have filled and subdued the earth. The filthy factories, the mighty skyscrapers, the boastful monuments, the cruel weapons—all are in for "the day of the Lord," a day of destructive devotion. The rest of what humans have made—our cars, our clothes, our computers, our art—will be, in some way, devoted to God, represented in heaven, and part of our eternal cultural lives.

Heaven will be a cultural place. We will again interact with other people, designing things, trading things, keeping traditions, enjoying a vibrant cultural life. "The contents of the City will be more akin to our present cultural patterns than is usually acknowledged in discussions of the afterlife," Mouw writes. As he explained to me in an interview, "The fruits of culture will be gathered into the Holy City, and I want to emphasize: none of this was wasted, none of this is irrelevant to God. . . . Somehow it's going to count for the gathering in of all the new creation."

Heaven will be full of culture, because culture making— properly devoted—glorifies God, and because culture is inherent to how humans experience life on the earth. Putting humans on a new earth without culture would be like placing a fish in an empty fishbowl. It would be so disorienting and so foreign to how we were made to live that it would be unhuman, just like a waterless heaven for a fish would be unfish-like. This is not to say that we deserve a certain kind of heaven—our corruption of culture was reason enough for God to rid the earth of us and our culture. But because of his holy stubbornness and grace, God insists on keeping culture, purifying it, devoting it, and getting glory from it forever in heaven.

In heaven, culture will be the way it was supposed to be. Swords will no longer be swords; they will now be plowshares. The ships of Tarshish and the Coca-Cola corporation will no longer worship profit and be bragging rights for their bosses; they will help humans cultivate the new earth for the sake of beauty and goodness. Movie theaters will no longer degrade humans and their bodies in tasteless displays of sex and violence; they will evoke awe of the human body as a temple of

God, fearfully and wonderfully made. Social patterns and traditions that once oppressed women and minority cultures will now affirm equality and the flourishing of everyone's skills and gifts. Imagine all the ways humans used culture to mess up *shalom*, the right alignment of things and of relationships, and imagine God taking it all and setting it right, an awesome and eternal act of destructive devotion, of cataclysmic consecration.

This is not to suggest that heaven will be fully familiar to us. Its social patterns and its cultural products will have some sort of similarity to what we know now, but this does not mean that walking down the street in heaven will be exactly like walking down the street today. A place of perfect *shalom*, a place that glistens with the glory of the right relationship among everything, a place that has gone through God's destructive devotion, is incomprehensible and unforeseeable. As Paul says in 1 Corinthians 2, quoting Isaiah 64, " 'No eye has seen, no ear has heard, no mind has conceived' what God has prepared for those who love him."

But as dazzling and overwhelming as it will be, heaven will probably not be fully unfamiliar. In some way, the cultural content, the substance and activity of our current human existence will go on in a glorified way. The "symphony of human culture," as Schultze calls it, will play on. We will not go from a life of energy to a life of vacancy. While the souls who are currently in heaven may be idle now (more on this in chap. 6), human existence will again explode with abundant activity when heaven comes to earth. "Heaven won't *diminish* but rather will *enhance* the values and experiences we enjoy on earth," writes Arthur Roberts. "Picturing heavenly existence as shadowy compared to earthly existence misses the crux of . . . a hope that offers something *more* substantial than what we experience in this life."

It was this point that made a lifelong impact on me when I read it in Mouw's *When the Kings Come Marching In*. It changed the outlook of my faith and the big picture of my life. When I first read it back in high school, I made a mark by this passage, copied it down onto notebook paper, and later typed it into my computer. These were the words that lit a light bulb over my head:

> If we think of the future life as a disembodied existence in an ethereal realm—which is not, I have suggested, our ultimate goal—then it is difficult to think of our present cultural affairs as in any sense a positive preparation for heavenly existence. But if we think of the future life in terms of inhabiting a Heavenly City, we have grounds for looking for some patterns of continuity between our present lives and the life to come. The Bible, I think, encourages us to think in these terms.

My friend Nathan summed up this point perfectly in an e-mail to me. A cultural vision of heaven, he said, "gives us something to aim for."

This tendency of God to salvage should not surprise us. The same pattern plays out in the prophecy of the purification of the earth in 2 Peter 3. Peter says that the earth will not disappear but will undergo a holy transformation that shakes it to its core. God salvages creation and makes it even better than before. God refuses to give up when things go wrong; he intervenes through Christ to rescue and restore *shalom*, the right alignment of everything. He does this with planet earth, he does this with the human beings he saves, and he does this with culture.

It is a powerful thought that God's power reaches to the places and things we consider unholy and unsalvageable. This is what perplexed Jonah in his escape from God. It's ironic that Jonah was on his way to Tarshish when he was thrown overboard and swallowed. When we see the ships of Tarshish sail into the heavenly city, it's as though God is saying, "Go ahead, try to flee from me. I will bring you, your goods, and your plans back to me forever."

Jonah had a hard time with this. He couldn't accept that God had the patience to try to save the worst examples of human pride and rebellion. He admitted to God that the reason he tried to flee was that he didn't really want God to save Nineveh. He wanted Nineveh to taste punishing judgment. "That is why I was so quick to flee to Tarshish," he says to God in Jonah 4. "I knew that you are a gracious and compassionate God . . . a God who relents from sending calamity." Jonah was holding out for a pox on Nineveh, not an intervention. He wanted Nineveh destroyed, not devoted.

We sometimes have similar thoughts about the prideful powers of our day, the oppressive governments, the greedy salespeople, the deadly weapons. We may not long all that earnestly for God to intervene and transform them and make them devoted, now or ever. Would Isaiah's audience have objected if God had said, "Don't worry, I'm going to shatter all the ships of Tarshish, and you'll never see them again"? Would we object if God were to say, "Don't worry, I'm going to take all evil things and institutions and wipe them off the face of the earth"?

But there is startling symbolism in God's act of putting the glories of pagan culture in his heavenly city. God finds it less worthwhile to eliminate cultural artifacts than to humble them. Humans can try all they want to make things to glorify themselves; God will only take them and turn them to his glory. The basketball star Shaquille O'Neal wears a tattoo on his shoulder that says, "The World Is Mine." Imagine God peeling that tattoo off Shaq's shoulder someday and putting it on his own shoulder, and saying, "No, the world is *mine*."

There isn't any idol so proud that God can't humiliate and turn into a humble servant. He can breathe down his fire of judgment and devote the idol to him, including it as a part of the flourishing of righteousness forever in heaven. The challenge for all of us Jonahs, then, may be to accept this fact and to learn to see culture the way God does.

To understand how hard this is, it is worth defending Jonah's objection, and ours. The reason it's hard to see the ships of Tarshish sail into the heavenly city alongside other symbols of pagan pride, even if they are transformed, may be because one New Testament verse keeps ringing our ears: "Do not love the world or anything in the world. If anyone loves the world, the love of the Father is not in him" (1 John 2:15). Aren't the ships of Tarshish "in the world," and isn't it wrong to "love" them? What business do they have, then, sailing into the heavenly city?

This discomfort lies at the root of the hands-off religion of many Christians. We tend to think of churches and our inner spiritual being as holy places. The rest of the planet, and everything we have filled it with, seem unholy and impure by comparison. This gives us a timidity toward being in the world, as one Sunday school song I used to sing expressed it: "Oh be careful little eyes what you see . . . Oh be careful little hands what you touch," and so on. Religion has always been on its guard against anything that seems worldly. Churches and souls are holy, but everything else is worldly. Being a minister, teacher, or nurse is holy, but being a politician or businessperson is worldly. Thinking about God is holy, but thinking about anything else is worldly. Heaven is holy; the earth is worldly.

But these are artificial and unreliable distinctions. Read the verses in 1 John 2 that follow the command, "Do not love the world or anything in the world." Verses 16 and 17 define what "anything in the world" is: "For everything in the world—the cravings of the sinful man, the lust of his eyes, and the boasting of what he has and does—comes not from the Father but from the world. The world and its desires will pass away, but the man who does the will of God lives forever."

This puts a different spin on what it means to be worldly. There is nothing about worldly places or things here. There is only worldly pride, worldly lust, worldly cravings, worldly desires. Other texts condemning worldliness use the word the same way: "Do not conform any longer to the pattern of this world, but be transformed by the renewing of your mind" (Rom. 12); "You kill and covet . . . you quarrel and fight. . . . [and] spend what you get on your pleasures. . . . You adulterous people, don't you know that friendship with the world is hatred toward God?" (James 4). Other passages tell believers not to be "polluted by the world" (James 1), or to "live by the standards of this world" (2 Cor. 10), or to accept "the foolishness of the world" (1 Cor. 1).

Over and over in the New Testament, "the world" indicates human patterns of pride, folly, and corruption on the earth. The Bible doesn't focus on which places are worldly and which are not, which activities are worldly and which are not, which clothes or songs or jobs are worldly and which are not. Worldly is always what's in your heart and what's on your mind.

Those of us who grew up in religious communities know this is not how organized religion has historically looked at things. Religious discipline tends to focus on where you are and what you are doing, not how you're doing it. For many years, the religious community in which I grew up had forbidden dancing and watching movies. Some religious communities still do. The assumption was that these were worldly activities, and dance floors and movie theaters were worldly places, and avoiding them could bring about holiness by default. But the most that these rules (which, I'm glad, were relaxed by the time I was born) seemed to accomplish was to engender a pious feeling of separation among believers who kept them and a heavy sense of guilt among believers who broke them.

There are many problems on the surface with this style of do-this-and-don't-do-that religion. First, it can give believers a false sense of security that they can be holy merely by not being worldly. In truth, sin can fester in the soul, the home, the church, and other nonworldly places—there is no safety zone. As I heard Eugene Peterson say, perhaps mindful of the abuse of power and sexuality by church leaders that had been in the news at the time, "The devil does some of his best work behind stained glass." So being unworldly in the historical sense is no guarantee of being holy. C. S. Lewis noticed that "the New Testament has lots to say about self-denial, but not about self-denial as an end to itself."

Another problem is that pious separation isn't a form of holiness as much as it is a form of fear and pride—the compulsive fear of doing something considered worldly and the pride of congratulating ourselves for not being worldly. But fear and pride are the very "patterns of this world" the Bible tells us to put aside in favor of humble confidence and freely flowing gratitude.

None of this should suggest that God is soft on worldliness, only that we need a better understanding of what worldliness is. Isaiah's hearers may have been surprised to hear that the ships of Tarshish would sail into the heavenly city, but if hearing that

prophecy led them to covet the wealth or worship the magnificence of the Tarshish trading empire, they had entirely missed
the point. To interpret the prophesied presence of the ships of
Tarshish in the heavenly city by assuming that God isn't that
bothered by the worldly empires they represented would be a
gross misinterpretation. For that reason, maybe there should
always be—to some small extent, in proper proportion—a little Jonah in all of us. Mouw put it much better than I can:

> Simply to "affirm" the ships of Tarshish and the cedars of
> Lebanon as they presently exist would be to miss the half of Isa-
> iah's message that expresses judgment. . . . God's people are not
> to covet the possessions of pagan neighbors. They must not envy
> the material wealth, the precious metals, the horses and chariots,
> the vessels of trade and war, the military fortifications that their
> neighbors boast about. To covet such items would be to show an
> insensitivity to the idolatrous functions of those instruments in
> their pagan cultural contexts. . . . And so, whenever God's peo-
> ple are tempted to look for security from a source other than
> God's protecting Spirit—or whenever they are inclined to "sup-
> plement" the power of God with military or technological
> means—they are condemned by the prophets.

The problem, Mouw affirms, is not these cultural objects but the
envy, the coveting, the misplaced sense of security that the objects
arouse. Against those functions of culture, God has a day of judgment in store. For the pride of this world, the abuse of power, the
self-reliance and self-indulgence, the lack of love and concern for
the neighbor and the needy, the nursing of grudges, the harsh
word, the violent deed, the gratification of lust, the disruption of
shalom—against all of these things, God is planning a fiery finish.
These worldly ways will perish, and all of creation and human culture will at last be free of them.

Until then, sanctimonious withdrawal from current culture is not in line with Scripture. I love how Robert McAfee Brown articulates this. "God's message is never: Turn away from this sinful world and find me somewhere else," he says. "God's message is always: Immerse yourselves in this sinful world that so desperately needs words and acts of healing, and you will find you are not alone, for I am already there, summoning you to help me." Christians are not supposed to be the ones who are constantly trying to dust the dirt of the world off their sleeves—they are the ones who are supposed to be rolling them up.

Granted, it can be difficult to fully separate the objects from their current worldly functions. To blithely stride onto the Wall Street trading floor and not expect to be overwhelmed by the greed that permeates that place is probably foolish. Believers may not be able, except by extraordinary acts of God's grace, to go to Wall Street and not commit sins of greed, or to take the dance floor without committing sins of lust. In this sense, the "worldly" do's and don'ts of my religious community had a valid basis, even if they were taken too far. Places and what happens in them can sometimes seem to go hand in hand. And so Christians may have good reasons to excuse themselves from such places, even as they acknowledge that there will be trading floors and dance floors in heaven. This is what Paul is getting at in I Corinthians 8, when he permits Christians to eat food that has been consecrated to idols but warns, "Be careful, however, that the exercise of your freedom does not become a stumbling block to the weak."

Our task, our tension, our balancing act, is to live in the world and not be worldly. To participate in culture—the ways humans organize, the things they make, the possibilities they imagine—without succumbing to the worldly pride and greed that permeates these organizations, things, and possibilities.

We rejoice in the fact that these things exist, that they came from humans carrying out the cultural commission, and that in theory they can glorify God, but we lament the fact that in practice they often do not.

We must be earthly without being worldly. We are on the earth and will again be on the earth in heaven, so there is no pretending—as Christians often do—that there are certain holy places where we are free from worldly pride and corruption, nor must we long for heaven as an escape to an extraterrestrial place where worldliness never was. Instead, we must prepare ourselves and our planet for the end of worldliness in whatever places we stand, asking God to transform ourselves and our surroundings from people and places of worldly pride to people and places of godly goodness.

That's what Romans 12 says. "Do not conform any longer to the pattern of this world, but be transformed by the renewing of your mind." The pattern of this world is warped, so start to warp it back. Live in a way different from worldly ways, think thoughts different from worldly thoughts. Begin to be a light to the world, a light of unworldliness in the midst of worldliness, radiance in the midst of darkness, as Christ was, and as 2 Corinthians 3 calls us: "We . . . are being transformed into his likeness with ever-increasing glory."

This transforming action—of humans, of nature, and of culture—is a central theme of the biblical story, and it must be a central theme of our lives. We seek to transform the creation, to beat swords into plowshares, to be peacemakers who turn battlefields into growing fields, who turn worldliness into earthliness. We pursue the radical transformation from rebellion to devotion. The ships of Tarshish will someday sail by the breath of God rather than on the winds of human puffery, and so our present response, in anticipation of this eternal transformation, is not to ignore them but to seek ways to start turning them around already.

When I began my internship as a reporter at the *Chicago Tribune*, I e-mailed Richard Mouw, whose writings on the ships of Tarshish in Isaiah had so inspired me, and said, "I'm boarding the ships of Tarshish!" I considered the newspaper to be one of the many human institutions developed in response to the cultural commission that had come to embody human hubris. It was a worldly empire; its function as an institution was to glorify the importance of power, wealth, and self-reliance. In the stories it told, it amplified the power of political leaders and business executives and idealized the material prosperity of readers. It wrote about worldly pride and worldly goals in worldly ways. The Tribune Tower, to me, was a ship of Tarshish.

I was young and eager, and a bit foolish. Since then, I have continued to lament Christians' reluctance to consider, much less board, the ships of Tarshish of our day, but I have also grown skeptical of haughty overeagerness to turn those ships around. For one thing, the ships are so powerful and have so much momentum that the efforts of one believer, or a body of believers, will often be met with frustration. But the bigger problem is that we often sail on the wrong winds ourselves. We are too worldly to do much weeding out of worldliness. How can I be sure my ambition to steer the ship of Tarshish I boarded was not itself tinged with the self-righteousness and love of power to which I objected—the reasons the ship was going in the wrong direction in the first place? The desire to take control can run the ship aground. This is why Mouw concludes that we are not supposed to seek the holy city of heaven "in any grandiose or triumphalistic manner." Instead, he says, "We are called to *await* the coming transformation."

But Mouw doesn't leave it at that:

But we should wait actively, not passively. . . . The Bible links its portrayals of the Holy City to very practical commands: pour out your lives for the afflicted; comfort the brokenhearted; love your brothers and sisters; feed the hungry. By doing these things here and now, we can experience something of the light of God's glory.

When we do this, we see a manifestation of God's work in the world that is not merely the sum of individual good deeds but an attempt to begin to correct the very winds on which human culture often sails, the social patterns that shape the human experience. "In [the] process of presenting and translating the word into the pattern of our cultural reality, our situation is necessarily transformed," Dyrness writes. "Patterns of creative efficiency in the work place will be more sensitive to the disadvantaged; habits of hospitality will become more inclusive; and relationships will be more caring and less discriminatory. . . . In all, pain will be lessened by a mutual bearing of burdens, so that joy may abound to the glory of God."

The ultimate triumph over worldly pride will come eventually. The recovery of the right alignment of all of life—nature, culture, and human beings—is an overwhelming project in which we can play only a tiny role and hope our own flaws do not ruin our efforts. Only in heaven will the destructive devotion of all human culture be complete. In the meantime, perhaps the most we can pray is the prayer my father prayed at my wedding: "Through us, may your kingdom come *a little more.*" May the eventual restoration of the reign of justice and righteousness be made a little more obvious by our lives, by the way we live in culture. But may we not forget two things: first, who is really going to triumph over Tarshish, and second, *that* he will. These two things are the last words of Isaiah 60: "I am the LORD; / in its time I will do this swiftly."

NURSERIES OF VIRTUE

Urban Heaven

When I lived in Chicago and went for a morning jog on the shore of Lake Michigan, I would survey the city as it stretched before me. My eyes would trace the forms of the Hancock Tower and its towering neighbors against the sky, then follow them down to their feet. There, one of the most scenic highways anywhere, Lake Shore Drive, restrains the buildings from spilling over Oak Street Beach into the lake, in a spectacular juxtaposition of city and water. In fact, the city's close encounter with nature seems to emphasize and even enhance its natural surroundings. To my right, cars whizzed down the highway. To my left, the endless expanse of blue reached for the horizon.

"Chicago never fails to take my breath away," writes *Chicago Tribune* architecture critic Blair Kamin, one of the best writers about the city of Chicago. Here's one of my favorite paragraphs of his:

> Chicago never fails to take my breath away. As I drive my son to school, heading south on Lake Shore Drive, I am dazzled by the cliff of condominiums along Lake Michigan—a body of water that is sometimes as angry as a gray winter sky, and alternately as peaceful as an aquamarine Caribbean sea. . . . We speed past Ludwig Mies van der Roe's steel and glass high-rises at 860 and 880 North Lake Shore Drive, as elegant as two men in black tie, and the curvaceous Lake Point Tower, whose undulating glass walls seem as liquid as the lake. And then, the squared-off towers of downtown rise like medieval battlements and Grant Park unfolds in front of them, a great green carpet that could be the gardens of Versailles. If you're not impressed by that tableau, I suggest you check your pulse.

From any angle, the sight of the Chicago skyline fixes my attention. The soaring buildings fill me with a sense of awe, wonder, and delight.

It is this sensation, Scripture suggests, that will be gratified to the glory of God on the new earth.

The Bible opens in a garden and ends in a city. The curtain opens on the Garden of Eden and, after the story of salvation plays outs, it closes on the new Jerusalem. In his vision of heaven in Revelation 21, John sees more than just a natural environment of grass and trees, and he sees more than just an assortment of artifacts of human culture. He sees a *metropolis*: "I saw the Holy City, the new Jerusalem, coming down out of heaven from God, prepared as a bride beautifully dressed for her husband." Isaiah sees the same thing in chapter 60: "The sons of your oppressors . . . will call you the City of the LORD, Zion of the Holy One of Israel." Each prophet foresees a cohesive center of all the cultural activity he describes. The ships and kings and goods are going somewhere. The energy and celebration have a focal point. The people have a gathering place.

Why Jerusalem? The name has important prophetic functions, urgent to the first hearers of Isaiah and John and instructive to the rest of us. Ever since King David captured Jerusalem in 1003 B.C. and made it the capital of his kingdom and the center of Israel's worship, Jerusalem has played a crucial role in God's plan. It has been, Eric Jacobsen writes, "firmly fixed as the center of the hopes and fears of God's people . . . established in the minds of God's people as the context for their hope," and it will "continue in this role literally into eternity." David's capture of Jerusalem made it the first long-term home for the iterant Israelites and the location of the first permanent temple of God. Its fall in 586 B.C. signified the alienation of God from his people. Later, the city was the site of the crucifixion and resurrection.

As important as this historical background is to our appreciation of apocalyptic prophecy, and as neatly as the name Jerusalem completes the story of God's faithfulness traced back to the Old Testament, it is not clear that the entirety of heaven will reside in the particular place currently named Jerusalem. When Isaiah sees the holy city earlier in his prophecy, in chapter 33, he is not trying to excite the Israelites about a specific place as much as he is speaking about the idea of permanence: "Your eyes will see Jerusalem, / a peaceful abode, a tent that will not be moved; / its stakes will never be pulled up, nor any of its ropes broken." Likewise, when Jesus tells religious leaders that if they tear down the temple he will rebuild it in three days, he is not talking about blueprints and construction; he is using Jerusalem as a metaphor for his kingdom. The same applies to the prophecy of John. So we should not become preoccupied with the connotations the name Jerusalem has for us now. We may instead see the new Jerusalem as a symbol of God's restored reign and as an indicator of the physical patterns of our heavenly existence.

Heaven will be *urban*. It will have streets and buildings, parks, paths, promenades, and plazas. It will stream with people and be filled with their interactions. Heaven will hum with a collective energy of cultural activity. Heaven's urban features will stir our souls, command our attention, and arouse our delight in ways that render our current cities hapless imitations. Heaven will be a place of wonder and fascination not only for its natural beauty but also because it will be an urban place.

Will heaven be one big city? Not necessarily. At least, not completely. There is no need—and no way—to know whether heavenly citizens will all inhabit one self-contained city or many different cities. Perhaps everyone will reside in a place called Jerusalem. Perhaps Jerusalem will be an international capital of many cities and countries (and read "heavenly cities" into "the heavenly city" from here on if you think so). Perhaps the name is purely symbolic in apocalyptic prophecy, signifying the presence of God in an eternal urban setting.

This uncertainty is not a major setback. When we speak of "the city" in everyday conversation, we are not concerned with exact boundaries. If we say we are going into "the city," we are not referring to city limits but to the sense of being in urban surroundings, among busy streets and buildings. We do not measure our arrival according to a road sign at the city's edge but by the sensory surge of the city's center. The same may be true of Isaiah's and John's conception of the heavenly city. They are not worried about location as much as the look and feel of an urban landscape, a dynamic civic arena whose activity gives glory to God.

Nor does "the city" preclude the flourishing of "the country" on the new earth. While the biblical story is one of progression from garden to city, the garden remains. The earth's population stands at near capacity, and yet only a fraction of the globe is populated. If the garden did vanish—if the last field were swallowed by urban development—there would be no place to grow food and commune with creation. The new earth, we can dream, will be a place of rolling hills, open fields, pristine ice caps, golden deserts, and lush forests, in addition to its urban center. Rural life will thrive. In the Old Testament, Jacobsen points out, many rural Jews called Jerusalem home when they sang songs of praise and made their annual travels to the city for worship festivals. Even now, rural residents tend to describe their home in relation to the nearest city—an hour south of Cleveland, just outside of Tucson. In the same way, the Bible suggests that an urban environment will be a unifying presence in heaven. In some way, heaven will have an urban nucleus. The city will be the hub of heaven's wheel.

This is a jarring thought when you consider the airy images of heaven that are so entrenched in our consciousness, as they were in mine. And so, as I wrote last chapter, we may find it comforting to know that eternal life will not be quite as disorienting as we tend to think—it will retain some familiar physical features. But the most important question about heavenly life should not be what aspects of it will be *familiar* and *unfamiliar* to us. We should not take comfort in the familiar or fear the unfamiliar. Instead, our most important concern should be *continuity* and *discontinuity*. The question is not where will I live and whom will I know; the question is how creation and culture will continue, and how the stain of sin will *not* continue. The next questions are, What continuous and discontinuous elements can I see in the world around me, and how does their future affect my present?

The same goes for the heavenly city. Having hope for heaven should not depend on knowing what things we will recognize in the heavenly city. The relevant question is, In what way will life in the heavenly city continue our current experience of city life? How is the physical place that surrounds us analogous to the existence we will experience in the heavenly city? In this light, having hope for the heavenly city means surveying our current social surroundings, seeing their sinful and prideful elements, and expecting and working toward their death. As we do, the words of Hebrews 13 ring in our ears: "For here we do not have an enduring city, but we are looking for the city that is to come."

When we do look at our cities today, the pride and folly we see is so pervasive that it can be hard to imagine any continuity between urban life on this earth and the new earth. Ever since the Old Testament, we have considered cities to be emblems of rebellion—from Sodom and Gomorrah to Nineveh and Babylon. And rightly so. Cities do indeed run on the engines of pride and power. They are monuments to human hubris, temples of idolatry. Saint Augustine wrote of this masterfully in *The City of God.* The struggle of the Christian life, Augustine said, is the struggle between competing cities: the city of humanity and the city of God, the earthly city and the heavenly city, the city of hubris and the city of humility. The call of God is a call to paradox: live in the two cities at once, physically present in the city of humanity, spiritually alive in the city of God.

I am reminded of this paradox every time I view the forehead of the sleek black Sears Tower, as I used to do on the sidewalk in front of my Chicago apartment. Built in an arrogant age of architectural gigantism, the Sears Tower was raised to glorify the city of Chicago—specifically, Mayor Daley's regime that ran the town at the time—as well as American capitalism—specifically, the corporation whose name it magnified. As the tallest building in the northern hemisphere at the turn of the century, it continues to call those who see it to share in its praise of its gods.

So the Sears Tower, and the city as a whole, is an ambiguous text to read. On the one hand, I am in awe of the collective creative effort it took to design a building that would rise so tall, and the precision and ability it took to make it stand so firmly against Chicago's ravaging winters. Such a wondrous undertaking draws my mind to the source of this creativity—to God, who gave the designers and builders the cultural commission to do this work and the gifts to do it well. On the other hand, I am repelled by the Babel-like boastfulness the building bears: the self-promotion of the government and financial leaders who wished to erect it to draw attention to themselves. The sentiment is the same one expressed by Babel's builders in Genesis 11: "Let us build . . . a tower that reaches to the heavens, so that we may make a name for ourselves."

The rest of the city summons similar ambivalence in me—part wonder at the collective creativity that speaks to a divine giver of the cultural commission, part sorrow at the haughtiness, injustice, and despair that mar these centers of human interaction. Writing about the earthly Rome, Augustine spoke of its *"libido dominandi"*—lust for domination. We see the same thing in our current capitals of worldly empires.

While Augustine called for a sense of separation, for patient waiting for the city of God while living in the midst of the city of pride, our current cities bear properties of each. "The city," writes T. J. Gorringe in *A Theology of the Built Environment,* "is both Babylon, the place of alienation, exile, estrangement and violence, and Jerusalem, the place where God dwells, sets God's sign, and invites humankind to peace. . . . Any city is always at one time both Babylon and Jerusalem." So what we do for now is seize upon the glimpses we get of Jerusalem and hope for an analogous existence in heaven, and seize upon the glimpses we get of Babylon to hope for the dying day of pride and injustice.

We may even choose a particular city as the place of this search. To me, Chicago is where I first felt the tension between the city of pride and the city of heaven. For Augustine it was Rome; for Dietrich Bonhoeffer, Berlin, and no doubt readers will choose the city closest to where they live or grew up. While I cannot know if Chicago will exist on the new earth, I have found it to be a good place to think about heavenly city life. Even the official motto of Chicago reminds me of the biblical narrative that begins with a garden and ends with a city. Every time I view the city seal, I read: *Urbs in horto.* City in a garden.

"Splendid Settings"

Along the north bank of the Chicago River rise the two exotic cylindrical forms of the Marina City towers. Resembling twin corncobs or stacks of pies, the sixty-story structures, made of beige concrete, consist of pod-like apartments that sprout from the buildings' central cores. Their visionary architect, Bertram

Goldberg, intended the buildings to be like trees, with the central cores as trunks and the living spaces as leaves.

When they were constructed in the 1960s, this was a radical vision to bring to the city of Chicago. The city was being deserted, and the downtown banks of the river were dreary and dirty places. Goldberg designed the buildings to inject some vitality and intrigue to dying downtown. His towers were cities unto themselves, with their own apartments, offices, stores, restaurants, bowling alley, parking spaces, and, at their roots, a marina to dock boats along the river. At the time the city's building codes prohibited such mixed-use facilities, but Goldberg defied convention and challenged the rules. The result is two of the most daring and delightful buildings in the city; arguably no others are as instructive icons of Chicago's commitment to urban energy and architectural imagination.

Goldberg's philosophy of architecture was that buildings should be organic and more lifelike and that builders should "seek the forms which give the most life to our structures." In Marina City, Goldberg left the city with two vivid reminders of the purpose of urbanization. Cities exist to give form to our social life. They serve as a "splendid setting against which human actions are played out," in Joseph Rykwert's wonderful phrase from *The Seduction of Place*. With our reading of the creation story and biblical prophecy, we can see the city as an emblem of the cultural commission, an outgrowth and embodiment of the creativity and communal patterns God implanted in human beings. The purpose of a city's existence and activity is to bear witness to the source of that creativity and energy.

The revelation that heaven will be urban, a dynamic center of cultural and civic affairs, causes our hearts to race as we envision the "splendid setting" of heaven. Heaven will be a place where things are happening and people are interacting. The energy of trade and parades is palpable in the heavenly descriptions of Isaiah and John. But unlike the aimless flurry of activity that characterizes our current cities, the heavenly city will be entirely devoted and directed toward one thing: bringing glory to God.

As we saw in the last chapter, this vibrant vision of the heavenly city contradicts our common conceptions of heaven as an interminably quiet place that affords little stimulation. These notions belie the richness of urban activity that biblical prophecy foresees. In the heavenly city, there will always be something new to see. Our current cities are evidence of this; they draw us in with their arts, sports, business, government, and entertainment. They are only meager mimics of the heavenly city; eternal life will be a sensory feast in a way we can only imagine. But to whatever extent we find joy and *shalom* in our current cities and communities, we anticipate eternal life.

Some popular accounts do portray heaven as a city, without registering the fullness and relevance of the coming civic experience. John Bunyan's classic allegory, *The Pilgrim's Progress*, has shaped the minds of many pilgrims with its telling of one traveler's journey to the Celestial City. Richard Mouw deals with this delicately in *When the Kings Come Marching In*. As wonderfully as this work has ministered to believers throughout the centuries, Mouw says, some of its features may be misleading. Our pilgrimage is not an individual journey to a remote destination. Our concerns are not just the virtues of the heart but also the virtues of communal life.

Because of the limited scope of these and other pictures of heaven, Christians have gradually lost the sense that heaven will be a social, interactive environment. The Bible challenges us to rediscover heaven as a place where the common and collective good is pursued in ways that witness to the harmony of *shalom* and the righteous rule of God, a celebration of diversity and variety of human interaction.

For North American Christians, this anticipation requires a new appreciation of the role civic environment plays in our lives. Our culture tends to idealize isolation and decentralization of human activity. We value "getting away from it all" and having "some peace and quiet." These ideals are understandable, but God cannot be found exclusively in isolation, away from the energy of urban centers. If we were really hoping for the kind of heaven that Isaiah and John tell us is coming, we would pay more attention to our cities, to their cultural amenities, their civic and community affairs, our duties as citizens, and our public interactions. To the extent that we do this without gratifying the human hubris of the city, we allude to the city to come. To the extent that we reject these biblical ideals and adopt worldly patterns of individual and unequal prosperity, we illustrate how the progression from garden to city has gone awry.

Emptying Out

The sturdy stone shoulders of Old St. Patrick's Church have stood on Desplaines Street in Chicago since before the American Civil War. At the time the church was dedicated on Christmas morning of 1856, it anchored a thriving Irish parish just west of downtown. It watched the great Chicago Fire blaze on less than two blocks away, and it witnessed the railroad revolution that ran through Union Station down the street. But in the middle of the twentieth century, "Old St. Pat's" was dealt a debilitating blow as construction of the Dan Ryan Expressway plowed through its backyard and shattered its neighborhood. Today, as cars race past the grand old church, it is easy to see the how the highway helped bring about the church's decline. Within twenty years of the highway's completion, attendance was down, and its neighborhood became a desolate pocket of drugs and poverty. Since then, the church has recovered; membership is back up and the neighborhood is being revitalized, but the parish can never be put back together. Now the membership of Old St. Pat's is nearly equally represented in every zip code in Chicago's metropolitan area.

These patterns have played out in many modern cities. More and more, cosmopolitan cities like Chicago have become destinations for travel and tourism, not places to live and to have neighbors and roots. The highway system in the United States, built during the Cold War to provide (supposedly) swift escape from nuclear attack, effectively gutted the heart of cities by enabling people to drive and live outside of them, out of reach from each other. Many close-knit neighborhoods, such as the parish of Old St. Pat's, disintegrated, and many far-flung suburbs were formed, collaring suddenly empty cities.

It would be a mistake to call suburban life wholly inconsistent with the urban heavenly visions of Isaiah and John. Suburbs are, in some ways, corrective measures to cities' absence of greenery, excess of concrete, and density of population. In some cases, they can be places where intimate and stable community life can thrive. But in general, the patterns of "white flight" from cities to suburbs are inconsistent with the vital, multiethnic, interdependent urban scene depicted in biblical prophecy. The values of urban sprawl—including individualism, isolation, comfort, and consumption—are opposed to civic vitality. As artificial environments designed with these ideals in mind, suburbs present many physical barriers to human interaction and the sustenance of community. Christian citizens must beware these dangers.

In *Sidewalks in the Kingdom: New Urbanism and the Christian Faith*, pastor Eric Jacobsen identifies the perils of the suburban lifestyle. He sees "an unbroken sea of strip malls and housing developments" and finds himself "disoriented by the lack of architectural cues that might direct me to the center of town or commercial hub." Suburbs, he says, lack "any evidence of human community." Ironically, although suburbs sprang up in the name of independence, Jacobsen notes that a visitor viewing vast look-alike housing tracts and chain retail stores would have a hard time identifying them as an expression of individualism—they appear to be the work of a dominant ruling body.

Similarly, Jacobsen says, society's worship of the automobile as an object of autonomy is fraught with irony. Thanks to our reliance on highways and aversion to mass transportation, we spend hours each week stuck in traffic on congested roads. We sit in traffic, going nowhere, growing agitated, not interacting with fellow citizens (except with hand signals when they cut us off in traffic). Highways allow us to make connections across great distances, but they tend to leave us disconnected.

As a result, we find ourselves starved of a sense of place. Novelist and city lover Jonathan Franzen writes that North America is characterized by the "New World ideal of house-as-kingdom, with its implications that what you earn and what you buy matters far more than where you do it." When I walk around the streets of downtown Chicago, I instantly orient myself according to historical buildings and other familiar benchmarks on the city's address grid that spreads out from the corner of State and Madison. I find myself face to face with other Chicagoans on the elevated train or the bus. In the suburbs, however, where most retail stores and blocks of houses resemble one another, I feel lost.

The problem with placelessness in our suburbs is that place shapes who we are and how we interact. Place is what anchors us to the earth and to each other. Public places are where we learn the virtues of civility, hospitality, and authenticity— Aristotle called cities "nurseries of virtue"—and the lack of such places tends to translate into the lack of such virtues. ("City" and "civility" come from the same Latin root: *civis*, meaning citizenship or, more broadly, community.) With fewer public plazas, parks, and sidewalks in our places of living and working, and with our appetite for the privatization of life— marked by the excess of our time that is spent in a car, watching television, or using the Internet—we risk becoming lax in our social habits, civic connection, and public virtues. Above all, we grow numb to the reality that we are preparing for eternal life in a social and interactive setting.

The danger of an overly privatized and pietistic faith is articulated best by Mouw in his comments on *The Pilgrim's Progress*. "When this partial picture of the Christian sojourn is taken as the comprehensive one—as it has been by so many Christians— the result can be a very myopic brand of Christianity," he says. "When the Christian life as such is viewed as a-lonely-journey-through-a-hostile-world, it is difficult to find a context for thinking about economic injustice or racial discrimination." But being blind to such failures of human interaction and interdependence reduces our anticipation of the heavenly city, where God's love and justice will dominate patterns of public life. It is these patterns to which we seek congruence, as a witness to the coming kingdom, and for which we strive against the oppressive powers that rule our current cities with *libido dominandi*.

With ultimate, if not utter, disapproval of recent patterns of suburbanization—the massive turning away from the poverty and ills of the city by the prosperous—we must rededicate ourselves to serving our current cities as citizens of the heavenly city. Jacobsen phrases his advice nicely: "We may like or dislike particular cities, but we cannot despise the city itself." He says that we must "learn to take our cities seriously. Whether we live, work, worship, and play in our imperfect cities, or even just cheer for them at a distance, we need to look to our cities if we hope to catch a glimpse of what God has in store for us."

And so, praying with eternal heaven in mind means praying for our temporary cities, amid all their failures to conform to *shalom*, the right alignment of everything. Jacobsen suggests that we pray for more sidewalks, public places, and public works in the physical environments we share as citizens. We must discourage and disavow worldly values of isolation and comfort as far as they obstruct human interaction and civic life. We must call our city governments and real estate developers to more sensible construction and development of our current cities, so that the words *city* and *civility* come closer to retaining their original similarity.

While it would be folly to try to bring the heavenly city to our current cities in any decisive way before the return of Christ—to vanquish Babylon before Jerusalem "comes down out of heaven from God"—we nonetheless look to our cities for clues of the coming eternity, for the joy of communal creativity and the goodness of interdependence. We seek to practice the urban habits that will eventually come to define our eternal life.

FUTURE PRESENCE

God with Us

H e was a most peculiar man," sang Simon and Garfunkel. "He lived all alone within a house, / within a room, within himself." The song goes on: "He had no friends, he seldom spoke. / And no one in turn ever spoke to him."

At the end of the song, the most peculiar man commits suicide, "so he'd never wake up to his silent world and his tiny room."

The bottomless despair and alienation of the "most peculiar man," and of everyone who has felt like this man some or much of the time, is the polar opposite of how God created human beings to live. And it is the opposite of what life will be like in heaven.

The third verse of Revelation 21 repeats the most important thing about heaven three times: "I heard a loud voice from the throne saying, 'Now the dwelling of God is *with [humans]*, and he will live *with them*. They will be his people, and God himself will be *with them* and be their God.'" With them, with them, with them. God with us, fully, forever.

If you read the Bible from start to finish, this is the most satisfying ending imaginable. The story of the Bible is the story of God-with-us, from its inception and then rupture in Genesis, to God's attempt to recover it with Abraham and the Israelites throughout the Old Testament, to the arrival of *Immanuel*—which is Hebrew for "God with us"—in the person of Jesus in the Gospels, to the descent of the Holy Spirit, God's indwelling, on Pentecost, until the final descent and perfection of God-with-us, here at the end of Revelation, for all of eternal heaven.

This kind of dwelling, though, is unlike anything else in the Bible. This kind of dwelling fills the entire heavens and earth, an unmitigated, all-encompassing presence. Heaven is one big mass of God's glory. There is no corner of it that God's presence fails to consume. There is no shielding your eyes from it.

This is the most important fact about heaven, and it is the most familiar to us. We already think of heaven as a place of the immediacy of God, where we will behold his glory. Compared with our limited thinking about the natural and cultural features of the new earth, we have the God-with-us part down. "I'll ever adore thee in heaven so bright," we sing. Still, since God-with-us is the principal promise about heaven, it warrants a closer look.

The most striking thing about God-with-us in Revelation 21 is how free and open and ubiquitous God's presence is. It wasn't like this in the Old Testament. To the Israelites, God's presence was heavily restricted and carefully contained within cautiously prepared, meticulously constructed places and spaces that only certain leaders could enter. It was like Area 51, the top-secret U.S. military compound in a remote region of Nevada.

An image from a book by Lawrence Kushner has been haunting me ever since I heard it retold in a recent sermon. Kushner says that when the temple was built in Jerusalem, the terror of the immediate presence of God in the Holy of Holies was so severe that when the high priest made his annual entrance inside it, he would have a rope tied around his ankle. That way, if he dropped dead in the presence of God, the other priests could drag him out without having to go inside themselves. It got me wondering: would my prayers—especially the ones I rattle off before chowing down—be any different if I prayed with a rope around my ankle?

Before the temple was built, the Israelites relied on a makeshift temple, the tabernacle, and that was even more precarious. You can tell by how hard it was to build. "Have them make a sanctuary for me, and I will dwell among them," God tells Moses in Exodus 25. "Make this tabernacle and all its furnishings exactly like the pattern I will show you." The rest of Exodus and all of Leviticus read like instruction manuals, going into tedious detail about rules and regulations. "Make the tabernacle with ten curtains of finely twisted linen and blue, purple and scarlet yarn, with cherubim worked into them by a skilled craftsman," God instructs. "All the curtains are to be the same size—twenty eight cubits long and four cubits wide. Join five of the curtains together, and do the same with the other five. Make loops of blue material along the edge of the end curtain . . ." (Exod. 26). And on and on, chapter after chapter of rules and regulations.

The preparations are so precise and exhausting because the task is so daunting: enable a holy God to coexist with an unholy people. It is like installing a nuclear reactor in a residential neighborhood—the reactor is capable of great power, but if its force is not contained and kept separate from nonspecialists, the result will be disaster and death. The Book of Leviticus may be understood as a nuclear reactor manual, an earnest attempt to prevent a Chernobyl-like catastrophe. I've decided that if I ever hear a sermon preached on a passage in Leviticus, I will hear it with Mr. Beaver's comment about Aslan, in C. S. Lewis's *The Lion, the Witch and the Wardrobe*, in the back of my mind. "Is he—quite safe?" Susan inquires. "Safe?" Mr. Beaver asks in disbelief. " 'Course he isn't safe. But he's good."

So the numbing detail of Leviticus is a testament to how hard it is to achieve the improbable metaphysical feat that God promises in Leviticus 26: "I will put my dwelling place among you," he says, astonishingly. God-with-us is a dangerous promise, but God makes it. "I will walk among you and be your God, and you will be my people." The nuclear reactor experiment is going to work. It's not going to blow up in everyone's face.

In fact, the point of all the restrictions of the Old Testament, oddly enough, was freedom. Even in this tightly regulated environment—or, more accurately, because of it—the Israelites experienced something of the freedom and fullness of soul that Revelation 21 foresees. Timothy Keller noticed that Exodus begins with slavery and ends with worship. The two are opposites, he says. "Not until you are bowing, ravished by the glory and the presence and the beauty of God," he says (and I love that delicious word *ravished*), "are you really liberated. Until you get to worship, you are still not free."

So when John foresees the perfection of God-with-us in Revelation 21, and it comes literally without strings attached, without ropes around anybody's ankles, without chapter after chapter of parameters and restrictions and fine print, it is truly heavenly. Heaven comes without a rulebook; it even comes without a temple. "I did not see a temple in the city because the Lord God Almighty and the Lamb are its temple," John says. "The glory of God gives it light."

The complete, perfect, unmitigated, unqualified, unfiltered glory of God, filling all of the heavens and earth. That's heaven. That's what we were made for. In Frederick Buechner's words, that isn't too good to be true; it's too good *not* to be true.

Because we were made for perfect communion with God, one of the main methods of self-discovery is God discovery. Understanding ourselves requires us to understand the image of God we bear. Most of what Thomas Merton wrote is startling to me, including this: "Unless He utters Himself in you, speaks His own name in the center of your soul, you will no more know Him than a stone knows the ground upon which it rests," he says. "The only true joy on earth is to escape from the prison of our own false self, and enter by love into union with the Life Who dwells and sings within the essence of every creature and in the core of our own souls."

This is a dazzling thought—that the divine Creator of the entire universe, a great and mighty being who exceeds the parameters of our comprehension, can in some way exist within the fiber of our being. He is not only near; he is immediate. He is inside.

Augustine knew this. His monumental spiritual memoir, *Confessions*, is written in such intimate language that reading it feels voyeuristic. "You are the power of my soul, come into it and make it fit for yourself, so that you may have it and hold it without stain or wrinkle," he writes. It's probably no coincidence that his request is identical to the psalmist's in Psalm 139:

Search me, O God, and know my heart;
    test me and know my anxious thoughts.
See if there is any offensive way in me,
    and lead me in the way everlasting.

Notice the word *everlasting.*

For a while, this reality seemed remote to me—the idea that the presence of God could be not only vast and mighty but also near and tangible. For years, I was mostly content to study theology and read the Bible as the story of God, but I could not believe that God could be *near*, much less inside. I could believe that he was sovereign over the universe, but to believe that, I had to believe that he was far away. I could believe that God *exists* but not that God is *present.* I could know God as a concept but not a being whose image I bore and whose essence I somehow harbored.

I had no trouble believing in God. I had all kinds of trouble believing in God-with-us.

So I admire a writer who has no such trouble: Anne Lamott. The night before her conversion to Christianity, Lamott writes in *Traveling Mercies*, she was overcome by the reality of Jesus sitting next to her on her bed. His presence was so palpable that she turned on her light to see if anyone was there. There wasn't, but still: "I felt him just sitting there on his haunches in the corner of my sleeping loft, watching me with patience and love, and I squinched my eyes shut, but that didn't help because that's not what I was seeing him with."

That's probably a preview of how we will see and feel and know God in heaven. Heaven will be the perfect place of God's complete presence. It will be where the God-with-us in which Adam and Eve lived and breathed in the Garden of Eden, the holy presence that descended on the tabernacle and temple, that became human in Jesus, that was breathed into believers on Pentecost—where this God-with-us will be fully restored and flourish in every soul and every square inch of the world.

This is the very definition of comfort, as John makes clear. The three "with them" promises in the third verse of Revelation 21 are followed closely—and causally—by the tender promise, "He will wipe every tear from their eyes. There will be no more death or mourning or crying or pain, for the old order of things has passed away." Sorrow will be banished. Death will be evicted. They will be impossible, because God's immediacy will have never been so immediate.

We sense this sometimes, when goose bumps bubble over our bodies during a praise song or when we are praying by ourselves and suddenly feel like we are not by ourselves, or when we behold the glamour of a sunset or the smile of a grandmother. We sense, in bits and pieces, here and there, once in a while, what this all-consuming immediacy will be a little bit like. But it is only in bits and pieces, here and there, because that is all we can take.

In between those moments lie some times that are as dry as the desert, as blank as a bare wall. I have known fewer such moments than others, but they have still seemed to be more than I could bear. And in these times the breath of God feels a million miles away, and the promise of Revelation 21 of God-with-us can sound like a fairy tale that will never come true. If the bits and pieces are the closest we come to heaven, then these droughts are the closest we can come to hell.

Because every human being was created to have God speak her "own name in the center of your soul," as Merton says, and because this is heaven, then there is no hell like silence in the center of the soul where that name should be. Because we were created for this kind of ultimate intimate communion, there is no awfulness quite like alienation. This was the reality of the "peculiar man" in Simon and Garfunkel's song, the man who lived "all alone within a house, / within a room, within himself." An empty room, an empty life, an empty soul. There was nothing he wouldn't do to escape this hell, including suicide.

The idea we have of a hell located in a lake of fire is nearly as pervasive as our pictures of a heaven located on a cloud. The true nature of hell, though, is not fire and brimstone but *loneliness*. Isolation from other people and alienation from God— these are shadows whose blackness is unmatched by any other form of suffering. It's the same isolation that made Jesus sweat blood in the Garden of Gethsemane and cry from the cross, "My God! My God! Why have you forsaken me?" Getting nails slammed into his wrists was one thing, but the thought of having God forsake him was unbearable.

So to ponder the eternal fate of those who are not reconciled to God—who are completely detached from his immediacy, and face a fate of eternal isolation and endless emptiness—evokes a horror that exceeds our dread of fire and brimstone. Hell, Lewis says, is being "banished from the presence of Him who is present everywhere and erased from the knowledge of Him who knows all." Hell is being absent from God's omnipresence. Tony Hendra puts it even more starkly: "True Hell," he writes, is "not that silly fire and brimstone stuff" but "being alone with yourself for all eternity. Only your own self to hope in, only your own self to love . . . a prison with no door." Fire almost seems mild by comparison.

Like our idyllic but misguided images of heaven, our images of a hell filled with fire, lava, and other tortures originate in the Bible. The Greek word for "hell" in the Sermon on the Mount— *geenna*, from the Aramaic *gee hinnom*—means "valley of Hinnom," a valley south of Jerusalem where the trash of the city was burned. As the Old Testament tells us in Jeremiah 7 and elsewhere, this awful place was where parents used to conduct sacrifices of their children to pagan gods. Imagine the shudder that came over Jesus' audience when they heard the name Hinnom—the stench of its trash, the thought of its constantly flickering fires, the echoes of children's screams from sacrifices in centuries past. Jesus could hardly have chosen a name that would have more horrific associations. Dante's *Inferno* embellished these images of awful suffering by describing the different kinds of physical tortures visited on different kinds of sinners, depending on what kind of sins they had committed on earth.

As awful as the images of Jesus and Dante are, they only hint at the true horror of hell. The endless pain of burning flesh is unthinkable, but it is not the worst thing there is. The worst fate possible is eternal isolation from God and from other people, a comfortless longing that never ends. In 2 Thessalonians 1, Paul says that "those who do not know God" face an eternity "shut out from the presence of the Lord." Another New Testament term for hell is related, as Anthony Hoekema explains in *The Bible and the Future.* The term is "outer darkness" or "gloom beyond"—as in Jesus' parable in Matthew 25, where the master says, "Throw that worthless servant *outside, into the darkness*, where there will be weeping and gnashing of teeth." As Hoekema observes, hell can't have literal darkness and literal fire at the same time. So these characteristics must be metaphors, and what frightening metaphors they are. " 'Outer darkness' suggests the terrible isolation of the lost, and their eternal separation from the gracious fellowship of God," Hoekema writes. He adds with understatement, "The imagery is to be understood symbolically, but the reality will be worse than the symbols."

Alienation from God and others means alienation from hope. "Abandon all hope, all ye that enter," reads the sign above the door to hell in Dante's *Inferno*. Hell will be a place where the restored reign of righteousness and justice—the recovery of *shalom*, the right alignment of everything—remains a distant and eternally elusive dream. Hope is the anticipation of a different future. Hell is the removal of that anticipation.

If eternal heaven will be on earth, where will eternal hell be? We don't know. Medieval tradition held that heaven was in the sky and hell was underground, but that was before our advanced understandings of geology and astronomy. The Bible doesn't solve the puzzle. Some are convinced the Bible teaches that there will be no eternal existence for those who are not restored, only annihilation. But this contradicts certain New Testament passages that describe unending torment. All we can say for sure is that the Bible promises the restored fellowship with God in heaven and the total, decisive loss of hope for restored fellowship in hell, and that establishing that restored fellowship now is thus proper preparation for eternity. You can't just try to be a good person, as most people, including some Christians, assume. You must meet the ultimate mediator of God-with-us—*Immanuel*, Jesus Christ. It is not easy to get into heaven. But it is simple.

Love's Argument

The opposite of isolation is intimacy; the opposite of alienation is love. The impossible but inevitable truth of God's immediacy is not only that God is near but that God loves. God-with-us means God loves us. You can't have one without the other.

The concepts of God and love do not seem to fit together at first glance. The idea of God—an omniscient, omnipotent being who is beyond time and other limits—as a being who loves, experiencing what for us is a desire, an emotion, a passion, and a vulnerability, seems theologically suspect. There is no other god in all of religion that loves. All other gods do nothing but rule. That's their job. What's love got to do with it?

p. 56

But God does love. "When Israel was a child, I loved him, / and out of Egypt I called my son," God says in Hosea 11. "I led them with cords of human kindness, / with ties of love." Jesus says something similar in John 10, comparing himself with a shepherd caring for his sheep. "I am the good shepherd; I know my sheep and my sheep know me. . . . My sheep listen to my voice; I know them, and they follow me. I give them eternal life, and they shall never perish; no one can snatch them out of my hand." He switches metaphors in a heart-wrenching lament in Matthew 23. "O Jerusalem, Jerusalem," Jesus cries. "How often I have longed to gather your children together, as a hen gathers her chicks under her wings."

These are not the words of a remote ruler. These are the words of an intimate lover.

But this kind of love, as the verse makes clear, is not just affection, not just a feeling, not just a stirring of the heart. It is an *inclination of being*, a tireless expression of intimate knowledge and joy. And this is the kind of love God created us to have for him in return. "Love the Lord your God with all your heart and with all your soul and with all your mind," Jesus commands in Matthew 22, and adds, "Love your neighbor as yourself." The verb for his command is not *phileō*, for brotherly love, but *agapaō* (the noun is *agapē*). This kind of love, *agapē* love, implies devotion, duration, and duty.

Our right relationship to God is *agapaō*, a love not just of affection and good feeling but of deep communion and duration. "Let my whole self be steeped in love of you and all my being cry Lord, there is none like you!" Augustine writes in *Confessions*. Later, he says, "My love of you, O Lord, is not some vague feeling; it is positive and certain. Your word struck into my heart and from that moment I loved you."

It is this deep love of devotion, duration, and duty that gives us a hint of eternity, a hint of heaven. As Timothy Keller argues, this love is itself an argument for the existence of an afterlife. When we know this kind of love, we know that it will never come to an end.

Keller notes the irony of this argument when you consider the way preachers and missionaries have historically preached about hell. They had it backwards, Keller says. Know that there is an afterlife, they preached, and get right with God. The truth is the opposite: have a relationship with God, and you will *know* there's an afterlife. Know the love of God, and what you taste will be so strong that you know it can never run dry. This is what Paul says in Romans 8. "Neither death nor life," he says, "will be able to separate us from the love of God that is in Christ Jesus our Lord."

The love of transient feelings fades; the love of devotion and duration never dies. This is always true of God's love for us, and it is sometimes true of our love for others. Think of a parent, child, spouse, or best friend. Your love for that person doesn't have an expiration date, even though the person's life does. You don't calculate that since so-and-so's life expectancy is such-and-such, you will love them until they are that old and no longer. It doesn't work that way. The love you have for them—not always your good feelings about them, but your inclination of being toward them—is something you feel down to your toes and don't want to disappear. So death—its agony, if not its arrival—always comes as a shock. No matter the circumstances, it always feels unfair.

That's a clue that heaven is coming. Buechner puts it better: "When you are with somebody you love, you have little if any sense of the passage of time, and you also have, in the fullest sense of the phrase, a *good* time." Then he ties this to heaven: "When you are with God, you have something like the same experience. The biblical term for the experience is eternal life."

If our love, our inclination of being, is as strong as we experience, imagine what that kind of love is like for God. Keller's assurance of God's love is especially sweet: "If God loves me at least as much as I love other human beings, then he does not want this to ever stop. He does not want this to get in the past tense. God will never let this go."

Jesus backs this up in Matthew 22. I wonder if it's a coincidence that he makes his statement right before he gives the greatest commandment to "Love the Lord your God with all your heart and with all your soul and with all your mind." Just before that, Jesus states that God is the "God of Abraham, the God of Isaac, the God of Jacob," and "he is not the God of the dead but the God of the living." So these people, and all people God has restored to his fellowship but whose bodies have died, have not fallen off the face of the earth but have entered into eternal existence, a state of God-with-us that cannot be shaken but will someday come into its own on the new earth. Keller sums this all up with a wondrous sentence: "The love of Jesus Christ," he says, "makes you eternally real."

So true love is love that does not die, and God's love means that the beloved, his people, do not ever really die. We still have funerals, and loss, and pain at the absence of the deceased. But those who know God's love do not vanish into thin air.

This is confusing. It is confusing to the child who asks, "Where did Grandpa go?" But it is even more confusing when we learn that eternal heaven will one day be on earth. Until that heaven comes, the dwelling of God, God-with-us, is not as *with us* as it should and will eventually be. In the meantime, where are Christians who have died, waiting to populate the new earth?

The Bible says little about what can be called the *intermediate state*, but some verses give us clues. "For to me, to live is Christ and to die is gain," Paul writes in the first chapter of Philippians. "I am torn between the two: I desire to depart and be with Christ, which is better by far, but it is more necessary for you that I remain in the body." I defer to Hoekema on this; he says the verb "to depart" uses something Greek has but English doesn't: the aorist tense, a tense that makes the action of a verb momentary and immediate. So Paul's phrase "to depart and be with Christ," in the aorist tense, does not mean departing the grave at the end of time. It means departing this world at the time of his bodily death, which happened a couple millennia ago. And this departure, which led to Paul's now current existence "with Christ," is better than his life was in his temporary body in a temporary age.

Paul repeats this idea in 2 Corinthians 5: "We are confident, I say, and would prefer to be away from the body and at home with the Lord." Again, the verbs for "to be away" and "to be at home" here use the aorist tense, Hoekema says, stating something that happens momentarily and immediately after death.

The thought of being "with Christ" is comforting to Paul, but it isn't his final answer. It does not reduce or remove the ultimate hope Paul articulates in 1 Corinthians 15, when he says, "in a flash, in the twinkling of an eye, at the last trumpet

... the dead will be raised imperishable, and we will be changed." When this happens, Paul says, "Then the saying that is written will come true: 'Death has been swallowed up in victory.'"

So being "with Christ" now is a good start and is "far better" than being alive in a broken world. But it is not the final condition of our existence. It is still an *anticipatory* state, as Hoekema puts it—a state of being blissful and yet aware that eternity, and the eternal establishment of God-with-us, is yet to come.

The deceased believer, being "with Christ," has a taste of perfect, imperishable existence and communion with God. But because of the prophecy of 1 Corinthians 15, the believer cannot be completely content with her current state, or the current state of creation, until the resurrection of her body at the end of time and the ushering in of the new earth and the heavenly city. How strange it must be that a deceased human being, who has previously experienced consciousness only in a body, with veins and nerves and a brain, currently has consciousness apart from the body, apart from her veins and nerves and brain. While this person is glad to be with Christ, the person probably can't wait to get back in her body, her perfect, resurrected body. This is why Hoekema helpfully says that the intermediate state is "provisional, temporary, and incomplete." It is better to be "with Christ," but it is best to have God-with-us back on earth in resurrected bodies, on the new earth.

We constantly get this mixed up. We assume that our eternal destiny is to "go to heaven when we die," like Grandpa did, and then that will be it. After the second coming, when we all go to heaven, up there in the clouds, then dying will stop and eternity will begin. I was looking for a sympathy card for a friend recently, and I found a card entitled "A Mansion in Heaven" (taking the word *mansion* from some translations of the Greek word *monai*, or "place of abiding," in John 14). The card read, "For he has built a mansion where his children will abide, free from pain and sorrow, forever at his side." That's what I used to think. Heaven is one big distant mansion that will host a big reception once everybody arrives.

But that's not at all what 1 Corinthians and Revelation say. They say that we, Grandpa, and God are all waiting for something else to happen, for the dead to be raised, for heaven to come down to earth, and for God-with-us to finally be complete. If that's what the Bible says, then that's what we need to believe.

Part of the reason we get confused is that we imagine a dead believer's soul as floating up into the clouds while his body is buried, entering into the surreal experience of being "with Christ" and being "apart from the body." It follows that we think of heaven as full of people floating around this way, and that this is the way heaven will always be throughout eternity. It may not help that Christianity has lyrical hymns about floating away to heaven, such as this one by Charles Wesley:

> Am I born to die?
>   To lay this body down!
> And must my trembling spirit fly
>   Into a world unknown?

The answer is yes. But again, the mistake we make is when we think that eternal heaven will be merely more of this intermediate state—one big bodiless, groundless, surreal, and solely spiritual eternal existence. As we saw in chapter 4, this kind of an existence would be so far from what we were cre-

ated to be—culture makers on planet earth—that it is no wonder the floating-on-clouds picture seems foreign to us and
does not inspire us to have hope for eternal heaven. But biblical prophecy makes clear that whatever comfort we have in
being "with Christ, which is far better" on a temporary basis,
our ultimate, underlying hope remains the return of God-
with-us on the new earth.

Although the comfort of being "with Christ" in the intermediate state does not satisfy our longings for eternal heaven,
we are still soothed by it when a Christian dies. It is sad; the
loss chafes. But the glimmer of hope we can have is that none
of it is final. In fact, for me, sometimes going to a funeral makes
the eventual end of death a little more real. Standing at a
gravesite as the casket is lowered makes the promise of death
being "swallowed up in victory" especially sweet, especially relevant, and especially real.

God-with-us and God loves us are eternal realities, tem-
porarily disrupted by disorder but never completely undone.
"Whoever lives and believes in me will never die," John 11 says.
I've come to rely on a word invented by Buechner to understand
this. He says the love of God makes us "death-proof." Obviously, being "death-proof" does not mean we will not experience the awful shutdown of our temporary bodies. But maybe
we are death-proof the way a watch is waterproof. The watch
will get wet, but when a waterproof watch is submerged in water,
it does not disintegrate and sink; it keeps on ticking. We keep
on ticking, too, when we are submerged in the river of death,
according to Paul. "Nothing can separate us from the love of
God that is in Christ Jesus," he says. We are merely "with
Christ" until "with Christ" gives way to God-with-us in its
fullest glory.

Community: Created for *Us*-ness

Chicago artist Deborah Stratman got on her bicycle one day and started leaving business cards at public telephones. She had fear on her mind; she was hearing a lot about fear on the news, and she wanted to know what everyone was afraid of. So she passed out these cards that had a toll-free telephone number listed on them. The number connected to an answering machine, and the recording asked callers to name their greatest fear. Of the few hundred people who called, Stratman said, the most common fear they named was loneliness. Many mentioned their fear of dying alone.

Some things never change. In 1890, there were fewer than two people per square mile on the American frontier, the line of European settlement, according to the U.S. census. Inhabitants of this vast expanse of land craved company. Historian Louis Fairchild writes of one woman who took in a guest and then woke her in the middle of the night, demanding, "You have slept long enough, I am lonesome for someone to talk to."

Loneliness is hell, and the opposite of loneliness is the opposite of hell. The opposite of hell is the heaven of nourishing, flourishing, all-consuming communication and communion with God and with other human beings. In heaven, we will have edifying and unending relationships with other people, filling us with the bliss of fellowship and the energy of their presence and personhood. We will carry what C. S. Lewis, in his marvelous sermon "The Weight of Glory," calls "the load, or weight, or burden of my neighbor's glory [that] should be laid daily on my back."

This is what was meant to be. This is what was lost in the rupture of *shalom* and what will be recovered for eternity. This is what was embedded in our DNA at the moment we were made.

We can tell by reading the pronouns in Genesis 1. After a litany of everything God created, all of the sudden he says in verse 26, "Let us make [humans] in our image, in our likeness." Let *us*. It's the first *us* in the Bible, and it speaks volumes about what humans were made to be, according to Keller, whose sermon on this passage has greatly shaped my reflections. Humans were made in "our image," the image of a community, a relationship, an *us*—a God who is three persons in one, Father, Son, and Holy Spirit. The doctrine of the Trinity is confusing to me, but D. Brent Laytham sums it up well: "God," he says, "is not solitary."

Because we bear God's image, neither are we. Like God, humans are meant to be in community, in relationships, as an *us*. "You and I cannot be our true selves if we're only a *me*; we've also got to be an *us*," Keller says. "Personal relationships, there-fore, are the meaning of life, the essence of our humanity." We were made to need human relationships. Without them, we can-not live a meaningful life. Philip Yancey wisely advises, "We have little guidance on how to live as a follower alone because God never intended it."

Our need for relationships is not just a need for company, although we need that too, as did the frontier settlers and Strat-man's phone callers. Our innate *us*-ness is something more, a deep-seated human need to understand ourselves through our interconnectedness to other people. "What creates in me con-sciousness of being a person is entering into relationship with another person, the 'thou,' " writes Paul Tournier. And so a per-son "seeks the dialogue and awakens to personal life when he overcomes his resistance and finds true contact with others."

Even Jean-Paul Sartre, the existentialist philosopher who exalted the individual, acknowledged, "I cannot know myself except through the intermediary of another person." Our individuality is so informed by our relationships with others that it is empty without that information.

The reason we need to connect with other people is that this is a way of connecting with God. The presence of others, in part, is how God becomes a presence to us, and not just a concept. Laura Truax turns a fascinating phrase in making this point. "Dwelling with God and dwelling with each other are linked because at least in part, *each other is where we find God*," she says. "How we treat others—our very orientation toward others—is expressive of God's life in us." And it is our witness to the world. In John 14, a disciple asks Jesus why he only reveals himself to chosen followers. Truax paraphrases Christ's answer: "This is how I'm going to continue to be made known in the world. . . . The love that you show among yourselves—my love living among all of you—will be all the validation my message needs. . . . Your love for each other will be the expression of God's life living in you." For this reason, Truax says, "Dwelling with God is an awareness, a lens that eternity has already begun."

Our relationships with people are, each of them, imperfectly, an analogy to our relationship with God. Because other people bear God's image, our relationships with them bear the image of a relationship with God. My favorite line from the musical *Les Miserables* is this: "To love another person is to see the face of God." This is why my wife and I had a prayer read at our wedding that was adapted from a sermon on the Trinity by Cornelius Plantinga. "May they be for each other your image bearers," the prayer said, "hearing your voice in each other's ears, seeing you through each other's eyes, feeling your touch in each other's hands, and reflecting you in their love for each other." My wife's touch is not just a physical sensation and a reassurance of her nearness; it is an approximation of what God feels like. Being with each other is a little like being with God. *With him*, *with her*, and *with them* is a meager sample of God-with-us.

This is why we crave intimate relationships—whether between spouses, siblings, parents and children, or close friends—and why the beauty of those relationships gives us a glimpse of the beauty of a relationship with God. But this is also why the unraveling of *shalom* in our closest relationships gives us our most reliable taste of hell. When we get close to another person, we make ourselves vulnerable to him or her. We learn to let our defenses down, because you can't put up defenses and have deep intimacy at the same time. In a world of unraveled *shalom*, we pay a price for this vulnerability, and the pain we open up to is the deepest we can know.

Just as the people who are closest to us are the people who give us the best glimpse of a relationship with God, the people who are closest to us are also the people who can hurt us the worst. A harsh word from a spouse cuts deeper than a cruel deed by a stranger. Gradually losing touch with a close friend creates a larger void than a heated falling-out with an acquaintance. Sexual abuse of a family member is one of the most alienating things a person can do, because it takes the act of heavenly closeness and makes it an act of hellish alienation.

In these dark valleys lie the seeds of hope for heaven. In moments of distance and disconnection lie the roots of our longing for a nourishing intimacy, an unspeakable nearness, a warm embrace that is not just a nice gesture but an act of consummate communion. Remoteness makes us crave relationship; lostness makes us long for love. Our temporary emptiness makes us want eternal presence. Meanwhile, the joy we have when our current relationships do go right makes us all the more eager for the day when God-with-us is reinitiated and every vacancy of the soul is filled with light.

This hope is very different from the hope of our society. We live in a society that rejects the fundamental reality of our human need for deep relationships. In our society, our connections with people are often distant and ephemeral. Our society promotes the sovereignty of the self and says that other people exist only as tools for us to use to gain more power or wealth. "Who you know" is useful only for advancing yourself. Talking to people is good only for getting what you want. Making yourself vulnerable is foolish; you must always be in control and always have a leg up on the other person. We are told over and over, as Keller puts it, to be a *me*, not an *us*.

This means putting on a front rather than seeking what Tournier called the "dialogue" that awakens us to true personhood. Unfortunately, society tends to reward our fake selves. We often benefit from trying to be someone we aren't and often suffer for being who we are. We must put on a false face to get ahead, to get a promotion, get a date, get a good deal. And so, conditioned by this pattern of cause and effect, we play along.

It doesn't help that much of our public life involves only the shallowest of our relationships. In contemporary life, where people move from place to place and prize their private lives, people don't get to know each other very well. The server in the restaurant, the client in the office, the visitor in the elevator, the driver in the next lane—they are all strangers we may never see again. Now that people no longer live in close-knit communities, as they did throughout history until the last century, they have lost a sense of obligation to their fellow person, and they have lost an appetite for the kind of self-discovery that comes from authentic interaction with other people. We have lost the "I" that comes from the "thou." Separated from our neighbors by our wide yards, our long highways, our big cars, our impersonal computers, we stay distant from each other, if not altogether isolated.

This is what we are trained to want. But we will never have hope for heaven unless we realize that this is an unnatural state of existence for humans. It is literally *unnatural*—against our nature. We were created as individuals to form relationships, created singular but inclined to become plural. We were made to relate to people with whom we become an *us*.

This is true of all people, not just so-called extroverts—those who are especially friendly and especially enjoy being with other people. Even introverts, or people who keep to themselves, have a need to connect with other human beings. "I'm not really a 'people person,' " I told a friend recently. "But then again, I suppose everyone's a people person."

In heaven, everyone will truly be a people person. Our need for other humans will never have been so obvious or met in such abundance. This does not mean we will lack time to ourselves or lack individual communion with God. Nor does this mean we will no longer be individuals. We will still have our own bodies and our own distinct identities and personalities. We will not suddenly become paper dolls, joined at the arm, one indistinguishable from another. But in heaven, the completeness of our relationships with other people—the *us*-ness that flows from God-with-us, will define our eternal reality.

And so while heaven will in some ways be an individual experience, our emphasis on individuality belies heaven's *us*-ness. This partial picture is enforced in part by the imagery of heaven from familiar hymns, such as "My Jesus, I Love Thee": "I'll sing with a glittering crown on my brow, / 'If ever I loved thee, my

Jesus, 'tis now.' " This personal pietism is only part of the story. We will indeed, as the hymn says, experience heaven as a *me*. But we will know it in its fullness as an *us*.

Perhaps the best—though limited—analogy that is currently available to us, that begins to express this kind of consuming presence and passion, is sexual intercourse. The experience of joining with another person to "become one flesh," as Genesis 2 puts it—the convergence of physical bodies and spiritual selves and the resulting sensations that momentarily overwhelm every barrier of fear and individuality that we have—surely this kind of connection begins to suggest the kind of connectedness we will know in heaven.

But beginning is all it does. "At the resurrection people will neither marry nor be given in marriage," Jesus says in Matthew 22. This doesn't forecast the dissolution of all marriages that were made in this life. But the perfection of God's presence, the restoration of God-with-us, will demand a higher expression of intimacy than the current practice of sex and marriage allows us. After all, the ultimate bond is not between a human bride and human groom but between Christ and his bride, the body of believers. Lewis says the pleasures we currently experience, sexual ones included, are a suggestion of heavenly delight, but nothing more. "What would it be to taste at the fountainhead that stream of which even these lower reaches prove so intoxicating?" he asks. "That, I believe, is what lies before us." Heaven, he says, coining a luscious Latin phrase, will be a *torrens voluptatis*—a torrent of voluptuous sensual delight.

Theologians speculate—and I am persuaded—that human relations will take on a higher form in heaven. The end of weddings cannot mean we will all be downgraded to platonic relationships with everyone—a sort of even-keel, passionless coexistence with no sex and no sparks. Nor, in all likelihood, does it mean that we will simply be married to, and have sex with, everyone. Marriage and sex, after all, are exclusionary—they tie us to another person at the exclusion of others. They create couples but not communities. A more reasonable expectation is that we will enter into a kind of communion with other believers that transcends any kind of knowledge and fellowship we know now. We will seek a deep connectedness with everyone, not in a romantic or erotic way, but in a way that nurtures longings for closeness, openness, and mutual nourishment. In our current life, when distance and differences make for huge gaps among people, even (perhaps especially) in the church, this is unimaginable, but it lies before us as the eternal *us*-ness that goes along with God-with-us.

Again, this is mostly speculation. The Bible does not address the nature of our relationships in heaven. But it does call the church, in 1 Corinthians 12 and elsewhere, to become a body as a way of displaying God's transformation in us and love for us. And so, even now, we have a vague sense of the *us*-ness of heaven in our communities, our churches, our clubs, our groups of friends. At its best, the joy of being with other people— enjoying them, enjoying being together—foreshadows the *us*-ness of heaven. It is as far away from the experience of Simon and Garfunkel's "peculiar man" as you can get. It is a sign of things to come.

So much of our curiosity about heaven, when we do indulge it, surrounds our relationships with other people in heaven. Will I still be married to my wife? Will I live with my children or my parents? Will I get to have sex? These questions are unaddressed by the Bible, and their mystery often impairs our ability to hope for heaven. But as curious as we are about these particulars, we must see the bigger picture in biblical prophecy about heaven.

The Bible does not talk about spouses and families—it talks about throngs and nations. It talks about a kind of *us*-ness that we have never truly known, a kind of *us*-ness of which our current arrangements of intimate living and public gathering are poor imitations.

The Bible does not answer our little questions, but it overwhelms us with its big promises. The first three verses of Revelation 21 contain them all: Heaven will have nature; heaven will have culture; and heaven will have God-with-us. Heaven, to sum up, will have the right alignment of everything and everyone. What more do we really need to know?

THINKING BIG

Connecting Heavenly Hope to Daily Life

E ach Friday night along the street outside my former apartment in downtown Chicago, the heart of the city's nightlife throbs to life. Young people wearing masks of makeup bustle in and out of bars and lounges; thumping music spills over their shoulders as they go through the doors. Smells waft from restaurants and drift into the street, where a chorus of cab horns fills the evening air.

In the exact center of it all, on the corner of Rush and Bellevue, a young man with a friendly but unsmiling face stands as though bolted to the concrete. He leans forward, propelled by an unseen, steady gust of wind, and, cupping a pocket Bible around his mouth, he shouts without stopping into the night.

"For God so loved the world that he sent his one and only Son, that whoever believes in him should not perish, but have eternal life!" Pause. "The Bible says, two shall be standing in a field, one will be taken, the other left behind!"

The man keeps on shouting, enduring the cold, the exhaustion, and the open scorn of passers-by as the night wears on.

At first, this man strikes me as a powerful prophetic voice. What a way to witness: to surrender your Friday night for the thankless purpose of standing on that corner in the middle of drunks and revelers, all for the remote possibility of calling people to repentance or even converting someone to Christ that very night.

After I pass the man a second time, awkwardly averting my gaze as I walk by, the opposite thought occurs to me: that this man's idea of faith and renewal is *small*. He seems to have found the most alienating way to talk to people (or *at* people), the way that involves the least listening, the least smiling, the least humility, the least possibility of getting anything but a cold shoulder in return. Granted, there's no telling how the Holy Spirit can stir and sway in unexpected ways, but as I walk by the man, it seems to me that our aim should be to remove barriers to the Spirit and open points of contact with the wider world around us in order to convey the truth of Christ.

The shouting man's methods, however, are in step with the small-gospel mentality that dominates modern thinking about religion. Like him, we tend to think of the gospel in terms of saving souls and making a personal commitment to Christ. Which it certainly is. But there's a lot more to it. The gospel is a mind-altering message that affects every aspect of life. Its story of redemption describes the history of the whole universe—and its future.

When we consider the full story of the gospel (from the Old English word *godspel*, meaning "good news"), we see a larger picture of the redemption Christ brought about, and we starve for the completion of it. The gospel stands on three legs, not one; Christ's redeeming work was done to restore nature, culture, and human beings. Now *that's* good news. "The total work of Christ is nothing less than to redeem this entire creation from the effects of sin," writes Anthony Hoekema. "We need a clear understanding of the doctrine of the new earth, therefore, in order to see God's redemptive program in *cosmic dimensions*."

In the terms of the small gospel, you make a personal commitment to Christ, try to be a kind person, and look for opportunities to witness to others about your faith. Which we all should do. But a gospel this limited also shrinks its source. In a small gospel, God's main job is to be a missionary coordinator, and salvation is an insurance policy for hell avoidance. In a big gospel, God is the maker and manager of the entire creation and the commissioner of all the culture making of humans, and he is working toward the restoration of all of it.

When we live in the hope of a big gospel, we see Jesus Christ not just as a serial intruder on people's souls but the one in whom "all things hold together," in the words of Colossians 1. *All things*—not just people's hearts but the infrastructure of nature, culture, and relationships. So the hope of a big gospel is not just going to heaven to be with God, but a vision of the new earth and the heavenly city as the place where God's authority over all of life is made complete. Living in the hope of heaven means seeing glimpses of such a place already, and wanting more.

In the conventional thinking of today's society, connecting your faith to your life happens mostly in small ways. Your religion is a private thing. It's something you do on Sundays and holidays. You pray before mealtimes, you keep a Bible by your bedside, wear a WWJD bracelet, give to charity. "Taylor, you're a Sunday Protestant," the pastor says in an episode of *Gilmore Girls*. "You come in, you say, 'Hi God,' you sing a song, and you leave." (Taylor replies, "I always leave a dollar!")

What the pastor is saying is this: your faith is small. This is a great compromise Taylor and many Christians have made with secular society. The authors of *Redeeming Creation* say this in humorous but sincere terms. "As Christians, we have accepted the secularist's premise that religion may be personally enthralling but socially irrelevant—that it is some sort of private vice, like pornography, to be practiced in one's closet." Enlightenment thinkers approached Christians and said, "Please keep your Christianity to yourself, safely confined to your inner spiritual activity." Many Christians responded, and still do, by saying, "Fine, we will."

Why have Christians been willing to give up so much ground? Why have we been so inclined to agree with atheists about the place of religion in public life? Why have we settled for a small gospel?

This is what N. T. Wright must wonder as he writes about the modern meaning of the word *religion*. "Whatever Paul was heralding as he went around the Mediterranean world, our post-enlightenment category of 'religion' is far too restricted to handle it," Wright says. He asserts that the good news is the news of a whole new kingdom. It's not just the successful abduction of certain souls.

It probably doesn't help that popular religious prophets tend to preach a small-gospel message. They have trained us to see salvation as a "personal transaction," as Richard Mouw puts it, a solely spiritual exchange between an individual person and God, which leads to a "personal relationship with Jesus Christ."

This is only part of the story. The problem is that this small story trains us to consider the presence of Christ as a natural fit only in the space of our souls, not in nature, culture, and human relationships. We see Christ as merely a converter, not the one "in whom all things hold together," and through whom all things were "created" and are being "reconciled," as Colossians says. Mouw's stirring words about the limits of the "personal transaction" model struck me when I first read them in high school, and have stuck with me ever since:

> Jesus came to rescue a creation that was pervasively infected by the curse of sin—an infection not limited to the psychic territory populated by "human hearts." The curse of sin touches the natural realm, reaching into art and economics, affecting family relationships and educational endeavors, holding thrones and budgets in its grip. . . . "Changed hearts" will *not* "change society" if the efforts at change are not also directed toward the structures and patterns of human interaction.

Christ came to mend and restore *shalom* in its entirety—every part of human existence that is out of place, everything that is not the way it's supposed to be.

Here's the extended passage from Colossians 1; listen to how un-small it makes Christ sound:

> He is the image of the invisible God, the firstborn over all creation. For by him all things were created, things in heaven and on earth, visible and invisible, whether thrones or powers or rulers or authorities; all things were created by him and for him. He is before all things, and in him all things hold together. . . . For God was pleased to have all his fullness dwell in him, and through him to reconcile to himself all things, whether things

on the earth or things in heaven, by making peace through his blood, shed on the cross.

The words *souls* and *hearts*, though used elsewhere in the Bible, are not used here. The verse thunders with the might of mastery over the universe. I've always wondered whether this was the verse Abraham Kuyper had in mind when he uttered his famous sentence in his inaugural address to the university he founded in the Netherlands. I adopted it as my credo when I went to work in the Tribune Tower in downtown Chicago. "There is not a square inch in the whole domain of our human existence over which Christ, who is sovereign over all, does not cry, 'Mine!' " Kuyper lived out this motto by covering more of those square inches than most of us do; he founded two newspapers, a political party, and a university, wrote several scholarly books, and served one term as prime minister of the Netherlands.

Colossians 1:17 is one passage that affirms Christ's claim on the cosmos; another one is John 3:16, though I only realized it recently, long after I'd begun writing this chapter. I was reading Richard Mouw's chapter on Kuyper in his book *Calvinism in the Las Vegas Airport*, and I realized how ironic it is that John 3:16 is the verse on which small-gospel believers base their belief that salvation is a purely personal matter. Mouw points out that the Greek word for "world" in John 3:16–17 is *kosmos,* meaning "order," as in, "created order" or "whole universe." Mouw writes these verses with the Greek word inserted (I'll use the Latin and English spelling):

> For God so loved the *cosmos* that he gave his one and only Son, that whoever believes in him shall not perish, but have eternal life. For God did not send his Son into the *cosmos* to condemn the *cosmos,* but to save the *cosmos* through him.

In the literally thousands of times I've heard that verse, I'd never heard it that way before, until Mouw pointed that out.

So seeing "saving souls" as the core of the gospel story is too small. The other part of the small gospel—having a "personal relationship with Jesus Christ"—has similar shortcomings. This phrase has come to be seen as a central tenet of Christianity, even though it never occurs in the Bible. Limiting ourselves to a personal relationship with God is problematic, for it focuses a Christian's attention on himself or herself. Robert Price states the problem succinctly: this personal model, he says, can lead believers "to focus myopically on the application of Christ's death to the private internal struggles of piety." When the small gospel is taken to the extreme, Price says, "the strong impression is given that God sent his only begotten Son, the second Person of the Trinity, to earth to be crucified and resurrected just so the pietist can . . . have a blissful quiet time." As a result, "the reality of Christ is effectively limited to a source for individual sanctification, even for spiritual coziness."

The irony is that while a small gospel appropriately humbles the believer with the reality of his own sin and the need for salvation, the idea of a personal relationship can amplify the individual inappropriately. It can bring a person to be so wrapped up in her soul that she loses sight of the relevance of the gospel to nature, culture, and human relationships around her. Price calls each believer to see "that her small planet is only one of many orbiting a greater sun" and "to see the same light [of Christ] that illuminates her shining on other people, other areas of life and culture."

How big or small our understanding of the good news is will affect how we live now in anticipation of how we will live in heaven. Take televangelism, for example. When television was invented,

Christians came to believe that the most holy way to use the new technology was for preaching the gospel—the small gospel of saving souls. Although Christ did indeed give his followers the Great Commission in Matthew 28 to "go and make disciples of all nations," Quentin Schultze, coining an amusing but apt phrase, says that when this verse is too narrowly understood, it becomes the "Great Commotion"—the frantic search for converts. "Although evangelicals have rightly kept alive the fundamental necessity of personal religious conversion," Schultze writes, "they have also sometimes tried to make such conversion the alpha and omega of *all* Christian activity in the world."

It's not as though Jesus said to "go and make converts," though that is part of the equation. Christ was calling his followers to attest to his transforming truth and let it work to restore not only people's sin-soiled lives but also the natural and cultural environment and human relationships across the globe. The small gospel, Schultze says, prioritizes the Great Commission over the cultural commission to the extent that you might feel guilty for ordering a pizza without trying to convert the delivery boy.

> Suppose we evaluate all of our communication—everything we write and say—solely in terms of whether or not the gospel was directly proclaimed. Most college lectures would be unacceptable. So would most musical recordings and concerts, mathematics, and engineering. In fact, if we said "I love you" to someone it could be construed as non-Christian.

Wittmer makes a good point about this small-mindedness and the term "the Christian life." "If *life* includes more than Bible reading, prayer, and evangelism," Wittmer says, "then *the Christian life* must include more as well."

Despite their narrow outlook, we must affirm that small-gospel believers often live with a palpable sense of the power of the dramatic transformation of Christ's truth. Even the man shouting on the Chicago street corner drew people's attention for his passion. They also affirm the important fact that you can't wander into heaven; you have to be reconciled to God in a decisive way. The danger of the big gospel is that it can get so big that it becomes vague and generic, leaning toward a New Age, wishy-washy feeling about the unity of all things. Big or small, our understanding of the transformation of the gospel must be centered on Christ.

But practically, a small-gospel vision can keep us from getting big ideas about what heaven means for us now. Imagine if the shouting Chicago street prophet lived out his passion for his faith and testament to Christ's truth in other ways. What if he stopped shouting and visited with some of the homeless people sitting down the street from him, listening to their stories and maybe sharing a meal with them? What if he devoted his life to advocating affordable housing or health care for the poor? What if he ran one of the bars he was shouting at and tried to make it better, or ran for city government to help bring about a more harmonious development of culture with the earth? What if he wrote songs that spoke to people about beauty and sin? And what if, in these ways of making culture and embodying justice and righteousness, he testified to the name of Christ?

Again, no one can deny this man the assumption that he was trying to faithfully respond to his convictions. But wouldn't these bigger possibilities make for a more meaningful connection with his urban environment and testify more powerfully to a God "in whom all things hold together"? Wouldn't they be compelling echoes of heaven?

The big gospel calls us to broad-minded ways of transforming creation and culture in the name of Christ. The Bible and its story of cosmic redemption should have us thinking big, and thinking ahead, to the time when God brings heaven to earth.

The future of the small gospel is itself small; since a small gospel stands on one leg—the salvation of human souls—its chief hope is similarly weak-kneed: the collection of these souls in a faraway place, the final step in what the sumptuous song "I'll Fly Away" imagines:

> Some glad morning when this life is o'er
>   I'll fly away
> To a home on God's celestial shore
>   I'll fly away

This is a comforting thought, especially to those suffering from disease or oppression. But it restricts heaven to little more than the assembly of these airborne souls "on God's celestial shore." A big gospel, with its three legs—the restoration of nature, culture, and human beings—gives us a bigger picture of heaven: the natural planet, the heavenly city, and the people who have been restored to God-with-us. The difference in this projection of heavenly sentiments, Mouw writes, is the difference in scope between the hymn chorus that says "It is well with my soul" and the exclamation of Revelation 21: "I am making everything new!"

The big ideas of the big gospel lead us to imagine a new earth, a heavenly city, and a perfected state of God-with-us. And they lead us to anticipate the restoration of all three by turning our gaze to our present earth, culture, and relationships with others, in addition to the reconciliation of human beings to God. To think big as we live our lives, we need to have a framework, a foundational vision of how heaven is coming to earth. We need a big gospel mindset for living on this earth and hoping for the one to come.

The Big Picture

Thoreau's last words, I noted at the beginning of this book, were to his friend Parker Pillsbury, in response to the question of whether he had any vision of the afterlife. "One world at a time, Parker," Thoreau replied.

To live in the hope of heaven is to live as though Thoreau were wrong. It is to live in two worlds at once: the world as it is and the world as it was meant to be—and will be again. It is to see shades of both creation and new creation in daily life—the present visited by the future. It is to see heaven creeping into our natural environment and social lives and to want more of it. It is to live with a constant consciousness of what David Dark calls "a world both beyond *and* presently among the world of appearances." To live in the hope of heaven is to feel the tug of the strange tension between what Oscar Cullman called the *already* and the *not yet*—the initial triumph of the first coming of Christ and the promise of his second one.

To live with this tension on a daily basis—to simultaneously occupy the two worlds Thoreau separated—requires a big picture of the world and our place and purpose within it. We need a big gospel vision for how we are living, what we are hoping, and where we are going.

"Ideas have legs," writes Steven Garber. Theories have their grounding in our daily walk. Neither is complete without the other—legs walk aimlessly without a deeper purpose; ideas are thought of to no discernible end. The way we integrate how we think about things and what we do with our days is a necessary but rare convergence that can energize the space of our lives.

Without such a vision, writes Gaylen Byker, "a daily shower of facts and opinions bombards us, but they lie unconnected, unwoven into meaning. There seems to exist no loom to weave them into fabric. Things don't seem to be held together by anything"—without Christ, the center of the big-gospel story, the one "in whom all things hold together."

Living with a picture of heaven in mind—not an idyllic post-card snapshot of another realm, but a vision of a world being renewed and destined for eventual perfection—means learning to articulate what this vision is. It means living with a vivid and relevant sense of *worldview*.

What is a worldview? Put simply, it's your view of the world. The connotations of the word, though, are more profound: a worldview is a big picture of life and what it is all about. William Romanowski calls a worldview "a kind of window or grid through which we see the world." It's a singular idea of how all the components of life—nature, culture, and humanity—come together and form a big picture. Not a picture that has all the answers—a naïve, mystery-free answer book. But a coherent picture nonetheless. Somewhere to start; something to build on. Something to direct our lives and give us hope. "A world-view describes the way the world *is*," Romanowski says, "while also providing a model for the way the world *ought* to be."

A worldview is a metanarrative, a big story, for our whole existence. Life is composed of smaller narratives—your life's story, a football season, a presidential campaign, the history of the United States—but we rarely try to fit them together in a larger, overarching story, a story of a world created, cultivated, and destined for perfect restoration. Living with a clearly defined worldview is how we can live in the hope of heaven, because it is how we understand that heaven is a relevant resolution to the present world, not an escape to an unrelated place and a totally unfamiliar context.

Living with a big picture in mind is rare in North America. Trying to define a broader perspective and maintain a sense of ultimate direction is an uncommon choice today. Many lives today run merely on the engine of aimless ego. We are told that the most we can do is to accumulate wealth and somehow make a difference in the world, as though any imaginable imprint on history were your best hope at defying your mortality. We can do better.

Still, everyone functions according to some sort of world-view, whether they know it or not. It may not be all that developed or detailed, but everyone has basic assumptions about life and death, joy and suffering, and nature and culture. Even atheism is a worldview. Byker explains:

> Mother Teresa had a worldview. Madonna has a worldview. The makers of *Star Wars* have a worldview. In the movie *Wall Street*, the high-powered stockbroker conveys his worldview to his apprentice. He says, "It's all about bucks, kid—the rest is conversation."

To go to work every day believing that you are trying to get rich to provide for your family, buy nicer things, or save for retirement—and to do this with the belief that the economic system you are under is the best kind there is—is to live out a belief in a big picture. To make or enjoy a Hollywood movie where the bad guy is vanquished in the end by the hero is to perpetuate a view of good and evil. To state that sexual fidelity is foolish and that you will sleep with whomever you wish, as

147

long as it's safe sex, is to utter a credo about the nature and purpose of human sexuality. Humanists—those in denial of belief systems of religious tradition—nonetheless got together and stated, "Man is at last becoming aware that he alone is responsible for the realization of the world of his dreams, and that he has within himself the power for his achievement." That's a belief system in itself.

When *GQ* magazine asked actress Jennifer Lopez about her multiple marriages, she replied, "I've made commitments to people and done things that I thought were right at the time. I just follow my heart. You do what you need to do at the time for what you need at the time." It sounds vague and evasive, but it's actually a profession of faith, a declaration of a moral philosophy that integrates Lopez's belief and behavior.

Human beings of at least childlike mental ability are incapable of separating their beliefs from their actions; they adjust one or the other when they fail to fit together, according to psychologists. So it's not a question of whether you believe in something or not. It's what you believe, and how your beliefs fit the world around you and the future in front of you.

You don't have a choice of whether or not to have a worldview; it's only a question of how deep and wide it is, how much it gives your life meaning throughout a variety of experiences and observations, and how it fits with the big-gospel metanarrative of Christ's cosmic redemption.

A broad, big-gospel worldview that connects heavenly hope to daily life might be briefly articulated something like this: God created the heavens and the earth, and he created and commissioned humans to develop this earth for goodness and for his glory. Humans introduced the invasion of sin and prideful perversion of the natural and the social world, a perversion we see and participate in wherever we look and whatever we do. The crucifixion and resurrection of Jesus Christ served to reverse the curse, to restore everything that was disrupted, a process we also continue to observe and participate in. At the second coming of Christ, when heaven will once and for all descend to earth, this process will be complete, and nature, culture, and humanity will glorify God in perfect harmony. We hope for this day, seeing signs of it already, anticipating its arrival eventually.

To live every day in the hope of heaven, then, is at least a six-step process. We must recognize the gap between what the world is and what it was created to be; lament that gap; realize that Christ's cross served to close that gap in part for now and in full eventually; anticipate this by starting to close this gap ourselves; be frustrated by our inability to do so in any decisive way; and let this lead us to long for God to close the gap for good with the coming of heaven, the return of *shalom* on the new earth.

Living as we do between the already and the not yet, we must live all six of these steps at once, every day, in every area of life. This mindset corrects our contemporary mistake of considering religion to be merely a private and spiritual matter, relevant only to the rhythms of the soul. Living with heavenly hope means finding ourselves and our experiences in this big picture wherever we go and whatever we do.

As citizens, for example, we must look for the gap between what government was instituted to be and what it is, perverted as it is by human pride. As voters, activists, and politicians, we must try to close the gap by participating, and by embodying Christ and seeking his justice and truth within the dynamics of political life (more on this in chap. 8). When we do, we will be frustrated by the failure or limits of our meager attempts, renew our despair over the prevalence of pride and falsehood as it plays out in politics, and develop a hope for the heavenly city, where government will function justly and truthfully to the glory of the King of kings.

Similarly, as economists, stockbrokers, or business people, we will see the gap—the void of righteousness and justice—in the structure and execution of the management of the resources of the earth. We will try to close the gap and will hope for the new earth, where resources will again be managed and distributed with justice. By going into business or reading the business news, we hope for heaven, for the restoration of economics. As lawyers and teachers, artists and athletes, parents and park rangers, we will find similar gaps, work to close them, fall short, and come to hope for the coming of heaven and the recovery of *shalom*—not as an *escape* from the wrongness we encounter but as a *correction* of it.

When I began my career in journalism, for example, I tried to outline a big-gospel worldview for my profession. With the help of Schultze's mentorship and teachings on the theology of communication, I came up with this: Human beings were created to communicate to each other to help them understand each other and their world. The invasion of sin distorted and impaired the truth and motives of our communication, so that we miscommunicate to serve our own pride. The massive cultural institutions of the media communicate to promote themselves, their celebrities, and their view of the world, distorting the truth about creation. Since communication is one of the areas of life Christ died to restore, we must communicate with trustworthiness, purely motivated, in ways that allude to Christ and the coming of the new earth, where human communication will again facilitate *shalom*.

This is true of all communication, as well as the profession of journalism. Christian readers and writers should see journalism as the process of telling the story of culture making, and what they read and write should register the beauty and potential as well as the sorrow and sin of nature and culture. And so Christians should read and write well-crafted articles and books on every imaginable subject, as a way of enhancing their God-given minds and connecting to creation and culture. After all, as our awareness of the beauty and intricacy of creation grows, so does our awe for the Author of all authors.

Abraham Kuyper liked to talk about "the little people," the everyday believers who didn't study theology in seminaries but still made their faith a reality in every part of their lives. I cringe at the condescension of that phrase, but I love what it's getting at—the fact that you don't have to be a scholar to have your mind and worldview transformed by Christ's truth. In fact, one of the key moments of Kuyper's life was when he visited a miller's daughter who had been boycotting his sermons. She objected to Kuyper's hasty adoption of the faddish heresy that Christ's body did not literally rise from the tomb. Kuyper was eventually won over by this woman's fervent faith, and he reaffirmed his belief in the physical resurrection. He later wrote of the so-called little people that "they brought me to that absolute conviction in which alone my soul can find rest—the adoration and exaltation of a God who works all things, both to do and to will, according to his good pleasure."

A man whom Kuyper would have counted among the little people was one of his countrymen, a farmer who loved to talk about theology. After a long day of working in the fields, this farmer, who had only a grade-school education, spent his nights reading works of theological scholarship, including Kuyper's newspapers and books. I've always wondered whether he ever heard Kuyper preach; I hope he did.

This man was Watse Bierma, my great-grandfather. He immigrated from the Netherlands to the United States in 1890 and bought a farm in Iowa, and one of the things he planted in his new land was his love of Kuyperian theology. I never met Watse, and neither did my father, Lyle; Watse died when my grandfather, William, was sixteen years old. But I would have loved to shake his hand and ask him what he'd been reading the night before.

This meagerly educated farmer became a leader in his tiny Iowa community for his vision of the breadth of God's kingdom, according to a tribute by Sietze Buning in his collection *Style and Class.* As an elder, Watse would often read the sermon from the pulpit when the minister was away or sick. In regular meetings of elders and deacons in one farmhouse or another, Watse held forth on the need for an American university modeled after Kuyper's Free University in the Netherlands, and eagerly described what such a school might be like. His sudden death put a damper on this dream. Buning recalls his own father's words on the way to Watse's funeral. "There can't ever be the university now." Buning says he didn't believe this at first, but he writes, "Ask me today why there is no Calvinistic university in America, and I will answer with conviction, 'Because Watse Bierma died in 1940.'"

Although he died four decades before I was born, the more I learned about Watse as I grew up, the stronger an affinity I felt with him. There was something about the image of that unschooled farmer poring over books about theology and expounding to gatherings in farmhouse kitchens that I couldn't get out of my mind. In fact, part of the reason I began my writing career as a journalist, I think, was that it seemed like a good way to live out the legacy of that farmer-scholar: to write about the world for a broad audience of readers, of various levels of education, about a variety of subjects that all fell under Christ's lordship. One of the reasons I've delayed graduate study is that I am loath to relinquish my credentials as one of the little people, a believer whose faith is shaped above all by what he reads and hears and thinks in the course of daily life and work—as this book was. My grandfather and father aptly realized Watse's aspirations by becoming teachers; my father is a seminary professor, no doubt Watse's ultimate dream. But I would submit my first few years out of college, working as a full-time journalist, as the closest I may ever come to living out the everyday, farmhouse-kitchen variety of faith in God and love of the written word that Watse embodied.

In his memoirs, my grandfather wrote of Watse, "I believe he was a Calvinist in the best sense of the word. He combined a warm piety with a kingdom vision that was remarkable. He dreamed dreams of a Christian university; he toiled in the community with tireless effort in the work of society. No narrow vision [was] this: he saw God's world as just that."

Some people say that the concept of worldview is an abstraction and a distraction that diverts our attention from the work of the kingdom to the thoughts of intellectuals. They say that worldview means to hold the world at a distance and survey it rather than to roll up your sleeves and redeem it. For some, this may be true. But the exact opposite should be true, as it was for Watse Bierma. Worldview is what integrates the work of our hands with the faith of our souls. Worldview is the big story into which all our smaller stories fit. Worldview is how we experience the reality of the God "in whom all things hold together." Bob Kramer tells Steven Garber that when he talks about worldview, he means worldview in this sense: because God is trustworthy and Scripture is true, therefore it speaks into all areas of life. And it not only speaks, but it orders them and interprets them. It enables us as God's stewards to be able to understand, to be able to make discoveries and connections . . . to look at social problems and figure out new ways of thinking about them. But not just to think, but making changes in structures and in society.

With a big gospel—the coherent, Christ-centered story of a world made, perverted, saved, and eventually perfected—believing in heaven is not like believing in Santa Claus, a pie-in-the-sky fantasy. Instead, believing in heaven is a relevant extension and fulfillment of our faith and our observations about the natural and cultural world around us. David McCarthy has a wonderful motto for this mindset: "Hope is the activity of faith in Jesus."

C. S. Lewis hits the nail on the head when he responds in *Mere Christianity* to the charge that heaven makes Christians idle and escapist. "If you read history, you will find that the Christians who did most for the present world were just those who thought most of the next," he writes. "It is since Christians have largely ceased to think of the other world that they have become so ineffective in this." Defining our worldview and putting it into practice can energize the work of our hands, our culture making, in starkly countercultural ways.

Higher Calling

Midway through the twentieth century, North America made for itself a new kind of heaven: retirement. Up until then, people worked their whole lives and died at home—and historically, death came at what we would now consider middle age. But as industrialization moved the place of work from the farm to the factory, youth and speed were valued above age and wisdom. And as life expectancy rose in the United States, the country faced a glut of older workers during the economic woes of the Great Depression. In 1935, the federal government instituted Social Security—paying people *not* to work—in order to get older Americans out of the workforce to make room for hordes of the young unemployed.

And so retirement was born. "The 'Golden Years,'" describes the Web site of one retirement planning company. "A time to play and enjoy new-found wealth. . . . Golfing, taking cruises, eating at nice restaurants. It's the picture of a long relaxing vacation at the end of a busy life of sweat and toil." (It's sort of a twisted version of Christ's anguished cry on the cross: "It is finished!") Retirement is a permanent vacation. Heaven on earth. When you scan the Web sites of retirement homes, a common slogan emerges: "A Retirement Paradise."

The problem with this artificial heaven is what it does to our modern understanding of work. As society keeps imagining more blissful ways to spend the golden years, its disdain for "a busy life of sweat and toil," as the Web site puts it, becomes more pronounced. More than ever, we see work as a curse. The *Dilbert* cartoon series captures the attitude perfectly: it portrays work as a mind-numbing experience carried out in dreary cubicles on behalf of uncaring bosses who suffocate individuality and make foolish decisions for the sake of fatuous efficiency. In the belief system of society, our task is to enter this world for about four decades, endure its monotony and the instability, and take heart in the fact that a slice of each paycheck is being put away for when you go to a better place—retirement.

With this bleak perspective, we look to the artificial heaven of retirement as the fulfillment of our existence, and our vision of the true heaven is warped even further. Accepting our society's promise of "retirement paradise," we come to conceive of heaven as endless septuagenarian leisure rather than as an earthly fulfillment of the work of our hands.

The problem with retirement, and its threat to our hope for heaven, lies in its strict separation of loathsome work from blissful leisure. Setting our work in the world on one side of life's ledger and the coming happiness of retirement on the other is not only recent in human history, it is counterintuitive to the way we were created to make culture on the earth. Next to the front door of the retirement home on *The Simpsons*, a sign admonishes visitors: "Thank you for not discussing the outside world." But to isolate ourselves like this in oblivion to the rest of creation is to miss the big picture, the one that ends not with shuffleboard but with eternal heaven on the new earth.

Living with a vibrant vision of heaven, then, means having a contrarian definition of what work is and what it is for. To work in daily hope for heaven is to see your work—paid or unpaid, for a boss, a family, a church, or a friend—as culture making in preparation for life in the heavenly city. To work in meaningful hope means seeing your actions as a part of the development of the earth into a cultural world of business, politics, education, medicine, families, neighborhoods, wildlife care—not for our own glory but for God's. To work in hope means to enjoy leisure when appropriate but to reject society's ideal of leisure that is endless and isolated. To work in hope means to note the gap between what nature, culture, and relationships are in a sin-filled world and what they were meant to be, and to work toward fusing the two, hoping for the final fusion in heaven.

Each person is created with unique skills for culture making and gap closing. Each person is distinctively created to fit a niche—to find the intersection, as Frederick Buechner puts it, "where the world's deep hunger and your deep gladness meet." To work this way—not for a paycheck, not in dread, not in the sole, shallow hope of the artificial existence of retirement—is to live out an active hope for the eternal restoration of the world. In this big picture, all kinds of work—highly paid, poorly paid, or unpaid—can be considered a calling from God. We tend to think of specific religious vocations—such as being a teacher, preacher, or missionary—as higher callings. But in truth, every vocation, every way we make culture on the earth in the hope of the new earth, is a higher calling, answerable to God. The word *vocation*, after all, comes from the same Latin word as the word *vocal*: it's *vocare*, meaning "to call."

Living with this vision of vocation means embracing the credo of Martin Luther: "There is therefore nothing which is so bodily, carnal and external that it does not become spiritual when it is done in the Word of God and faith." It means living with a big picture of nature, culture, and human beings. It means seeing that the elements of work—creativity, problem solving, cooperation, physical or mental stimulation, satisfaction—are godly processes, ways we bear the image of God. "Vocation in the most comprehensive sense," writes Steve Van Der Weele, summarizing the book *Vocation: Discerning Our Callings in Life*, "consists of one's total relational efforts and energies—every response we make in loving obedience to the challenge of establishing a functional, believing community."

While I was living in New York City and working as a summer intern at Time Inc. magazines, a copy of *Fortune* was dropped off at my cubicle. The cover read, "God and Business." I eagerly opened it up, and I savored what I read. "Why would we want to look for God in our work? The simple answer is most of us spend so much time working, it would be a shame if we couldn't find God there," Gregory F. A. Pearce, co-founder of the Chicago-based Business Leaders for Excellence, Ethics, and Justice, told the magazine. But he went on: "A more complex answer is that there is a creative energy in work that is somehow tied to God's creative energy. If we can understand that connection, perhaps we can use it to transform the workplace into something remarkable." David Miller, a former IBM executive and founder of the Avodah Institute, left the corporate world for Princeton Seminary, according to the *Fortune* article. "People often talk about the sacred-secular divide," Miller said, "but my faith tells me that God is found in earth and rocks and buildings and institutions, and, yes, in the business world." The Hebrew word *avodah,* Miller pointed out, means both "work" and "worship." What Pearce and Miller were talking about was the cultural commission.

"This is about who you are, your being, your character within the organization," Miller told *Fortune.* "It's going beyond minimum obligation to being motivated by love of neighbor." Thinking in these terms depends on how you envision economics in heaven, how you see your own part in building the heavenly city, and how you hope for Christ to bring that work to completion.

This vision of work as the building of the heavenly city takes Christians to unlikely and hostile places—even right into the heart of the ships of Tarshish, the cultural empires of our day. When Carl Dill went to work as an executive vice president of technology for the Time Warner corporation in New York City, he found himself at the helm of one of the largest companies in the international center of capitalism. In his work as an administrator, people who worked under him began to notice something about him that quietly stood out; Dill wasn't an assertive, domineering executive. A soft-spoken man, he carefully listened to what people said and encouraged them to voice their views. He calmly gave orders and patiently and warmly interacted with people as he ran his department. People respected him not only for his professional expertise, which was considerable, but for the person he was and the way he served other people—"servant leadership," as he described it to me.

Some of Dill's employees were moved to ask what it was that drove him to work in such a different way. In responding to these questions, Dill had a chance to name the name of Jesus Christ in a way he never would have, had his intent from the start been only to evangelize, to preach the small gospel. Had he shouted damnation from the street corner, like that man outside my apartment building in Chicago, Dill would never have gotten in the door at Time Warner, much less into a vice president's office suite. Finally, Dill taught his co-workers the ultimate lesson. Fed up with the unwise practices of higher management, he resigned his position to become an independent consultant. He belonged to no worldly empire, only to the kingdom to come.

"We can't and shouldn't and don't want to drive people to a particular religious belief," Bill Pollard, chairman of the Fortune 500 company ServiceMaster, told *Fortune*. "But we do want people to ask the fundamental questions. What's driving them? What is this life all about?" That's what Dill did. And that's what Christian college student Sarah Maxwell did as she entered another cultural empire, the broadcast news media. In her internship at her local NBC affiliate's news program, she worked her way up to weekend assistant editor, organizing reporters' assignments and writing news copy. "To make an impact on our culture, you have to infiltrate it," she told a publication from her college. "At my office, people often tell me, 'You're different from most Christians. You don't push your views, and you're not afraid to dialogue about difficult things.' " That's preaching the big gospel.

"People who want to mix God and business are rebels on several fronts," wrote reporter Marc Gunther in *Fortune.* "They reject the centuries-old American conviction that spirituality is a private matter. They challenge religious thinkers who disdain business as an inherently impure pursuit. . . . Most of all, they refuse to bow to the all too common notion that much of the work done in corporate America must be routine, dull, and meaningless: they want and expect more."

They want and expect the goodness humans can know from faithful cultivation of the earth. They want and expect the promise of grace when they see how the hell of human pride and injustice plays out in the structures of society. They seek what Jewish believers call for in their beautiful Hebrew phrase *tikkum olam,* the repair of the world. They want and expect a heavenly city, one that they are helping to build. They want God to and expect that only God can bring heaven to earth at the end of time.

As much as we need to recommit ourselves to a new vision of work, we need to de-emphasize work at the same time. We need to live with what author Arthur F. Miller calls a "detached intensity"—a palpable ambition for broad-minded service tempered with a healthy sense of balance among all areas of our lives, including rest. Even as we reject society's ideal of eventual endless leisure, we also reject its workaholism.

As contemporary life grows more and more chaotic and frenzied, in a society that devotes too much time and energy to work and transportation and not enough to peaceful rest, quiet contemplation, and patient, relaxed fellowship, we need to follow the model of Christ—who had a mere three years to change the world and yet repeatedly retreated to nap on a fishing boat while crowds clamored for more of his time. Rest, he seemed to suggest, will be an integral part of life on the new earth.

At one point in Luke 10, Christ tells his friend Martha to get out of the kitchen and have a seat by him, as her seemingly lazy sister Mary has done. "Martha, Martha, you are worried and upset about many things, but only one thing is needed. Mary has chosen what is better, and it will not be taken away from her." Lest we become too self-important about our work, Christ-like rest cuts us down to size and allows us to practice patience for God to bring about the new earth. It might, after all, take some time.

Paul Marshall helpfully describes this kind of balance in our working lives.

> As creatures made in the image of God we are called to do many things other than work. We are called to be Christianly responsible in all our relationships: we are called to be good husbands, wives, parents, children, neighbors, friends, and citizens. Our mandate and calling is to image God in every dimension of our existence—including worship, intimacy, play, and rest. While the [life of the mind] is not a higher kind of life, it too is an essential part of our life. Our work has, per se, no prior claim to our time.

Mouw says that Kuyper, that busy theologian, journalist, and politician, knew the need for quiet rest as well as anyone. He writes that one of Kuyper's favorite verses was from Psalm 73: "But as for me, it is good to be near God. / I have made the Sovereign LORD my refuge; / I will tell of all your deeds."

Living with a big picture of life and of heaven leads us to seek a sense of wholeness in life and in our view of the world, and not become preoccupied with certain tasks, causes, and minor ambitions. We know that making culture happens in a variety of ways, not just the ones that bring about profit or achievement. So although every individual is blessed with certain skills and specific callings, we all need to rediscover a diversity of mission, which the apostle Paul articulates in 1 Corinthians 10: "Whether you eat or drink, do it to the glory of God."

Robert Price skillfully positions this view against that of the slogan "God is my co-pilot." Modern society tends to see God as a spiritual trainer—an energizing, managing force that extends our ambitions. "It is [somewhat] like giving someone else the keys to your car; you won't be driving it any more," Price writes. But he continues:

> What if "giving your life to Christ" were more like writing a book or a song and then like dedicating it to someone else? "I will live my life in all its fullness, enjoying my interests, and making my decisions responsibly. And the whole resulting tapestry I present to Jesus as a gift, which I hope he will enjoy as I have."

To maintain this radical vision of dedication, telling the big-gospel story, and seeing a big picture of Christ-like coherence in all areas of our lives, we need to rediscover our heavenly citizenship and reject allegiance to the empires of the present age.

ALIEN AMBASSADORS

Living as Citizens of Heaven

Two thousand years ago, a man from Galilee started making waves with his radical views. He started to gain quite a following. He proclaimed the kingdom of God. He condemned injustice. He cleansed the temple. To shut him up, he was put to death.

His name was Judas of Galilee. We don't know much about him—what we do know comes from the historian Josephus—but we know that his life overlapped that of another Galilean radical, Jesus, and that Jesus had heard all about him. When Jesus was still a toddler, Judas of Galilee declared a rebellion against a new tax imposed by the Roman Empire, the tribute tax. This tax wasn't all that much—it was just one denarius, or about one day's wages for a laborer, according to Mark 6. But it may have been the most insulting tax that subjects under Roman occupation had to pay. The tribute tax was a tax for the privilege, so the Romans said, of living in the Roman Empire. A tax for being a Roman subject. As if the cruel oppression by Roman soldiers weren't punishment enough, now you had to pay a gratuity for it. It was cheap, but it stung.

Judas of Galilee would have none of it. He called on all Jews to refuse to pay the new tax and to acknowledge God alone as their ruler. No gesture, however small, was acceptable if it was a gesture of acquiescence to Rome. One denarius was too high a price to pay. So Judas stirred up an armed revolt. He stormed into the temple and rid it of all foreigners. He boldly defied the kingdom of Caesar and pledged sole allegiance to the kingdom of God. Before long, he was arrested and executed.

Today the name Judas is synonymous with "traitor"; calling someone "a Judas" is an accusation of betrayal. This is because another Judas—Judas Iscariot—betrayed Jesus in one of the most famous sellouts in history. But before Judas Iscariot literally made a name for himself, the name Judas was strongly associated with being a revolutionary. It began in the second century B.C. with Judas Maccabeus, who decried the secularization of Jerusalem and led an army to cleanse the temple—the event commemorated by the feast of Chanukah (or Hanukkah). A century and a half later, Judas of Galilee lived up to his name, leading a similar revolt to the same place, the temple. His short-lived rebellion ensured that wherever Jesus went once he started his ministry, the name Judas would loom overhead and be read into his words. (It didn't help that Jesus' name even sounded somewhat like "Judas.") Wherever he went, whomever he met, the question was unspoken but on everyone's mind: "Are you another Judas?"

Finally, in Mark 12, the Pharisees asked it out loud. And for good reason. They'd been listening to Jesus preach about the kingdom of God for almost three years and had seen the large crowds that were eating it up. They'd just seen Jesus ride into Jerusalem in triumph on Palm Sunday, basking in the adoration of the people. And, causing them the most alarm, they'd just seen Jesus cleanse the temple, flying around in a fit of rage as he shooed the moneychangers away. Jesus was acting just like Judas. Preaching the kingdom of God. Cleansing the temple. He was two for three. The only question left was his stand on the tribute tax, the tax that had started the ill-fated anti-Rome campaign of Judas the Galilean twenty-five years earlier.

So they asked him the question. "Is it right to pay taxes [the Greek says "tribute"] to Caesar or not?" It was no casual inquiry. The Pharisees weren't merely curious how Jesus would handle a hot potato. Verse 13 says that the Pharisees brought along the Herodians to hear Jesus' answer. The Pharisees, who hated the corrupting, secular influence of Roman rule, were sworn enemies of the Herodians, who were loyal to Rome's local representative, Herod. They agreed on nothing. But they agreed to cooperate long enough to set a trap for Jesus.

Here was their plan. If Jesus said that people shouldn't pay the tribute tax, the Herodians would march right over to Herod and tell him that they had another revolutionary, another Judas, on their hands. Kingdom of God, cleansing the temple, opposing the tribute tax—it added up to another revolt. And Herod would squash it like a bug, as he did with Judas the Galilean. But if Jesus said the opposite and told people to pay the tribute tax, the Pharisees would announce that Jesus was a phony, a sellout to Rome, someone who talked big about the kingdom of God but bowed to Rome when it came right down to it. He didn't put his money where his mouth was. So it was time to corner Jesus and make him come clean. Are you another Judas? Are you a revolutionary? Or are you going to chicken out?

Mark says Jesus' audience was amazed at his answer, so stunned that they walked away. And rightly so. "Give to Caesar what is Caesar's, and to God what is God's," Jesus said. It sounds like a diplomatic answer, but it isn't. It's one of the most revolutionary things ever said by a revolutionary, because, in the words of Timothy Keller, whose sermon on this passage I heard in New York City and has greatly informed my reading, "This is the revolution that revolutionizes revolutions."

The first thing to notice is that Jesus doesn't take sides. He doesn't pick one or the other. He doesn't have a political platform. He's not one of the Essenes, the writers of the Dead Sea Scrolls, who responded to the injustice of society by escaping from it and going off to live by themselves in the hills, paying no taxes, having no civic participation. But he's not a Zealot, as Judas the Galilean was, responding to the injustice of society by raising a rebellion against Rome. If so, he would have said, "Don't pay the tribute tax," and the revolt would be on. And he's not a loyal Roman subject, either. If so, he would have said, "Do your patriotic duty; pay your tribute to Rome," and left it at that. He doesn't choose one or the other. And when you look at it, Keller says, Jesus doesn't choose the middle, either. He's in a whole new category by himself.

The first hint of this new category is the first word in Jesus' conclusion. "Give," or, as the King James Version puts it, "Render." It doesn't show up in contemporary English versions, but this is a different word from the one in the Pharisees' question. Their question uses the Greek word *dōmen*, meaning to give a gift or donation. But Jesus' answer uses the word *apodote*, meaning to give back or return. Jesus refuses to answer the Pharisees' question in their own terms. And it makes his answer more radical than it sounds. What he's saying is that you're doing no favor, no obsequious gesture, to Caesar by paying his tribute tax. You're giving him his stuff back. It's not really much of a tribute.

It's not the tribute Caesar wanted, anyway. He wrote what he wanted on the coin. The inscription on the front of the denarius, which Jesus asks about in verse 16, read "Tiberius Caesar, Son of the Divine Augustus." The back of the coin read "Pontifex Maximus" ("High Priest"). Caesar, Son of God, Chief Priest.

Read between the lines of Jesus' answer, as the Pharisees and Herodians did, and what he's saying is this: "Give Tiberius his coins, which he minted from his own stock of silver. They're his belongings. But don't give him your ultimate allegiance (King), your reverence (Son of God), and your faith (High Priest). That belongs to someone else." (The Herodians must have been furious, but they couldn't have Jesus arrested—he hadn't challenged Tiberius's right to rule from Rome, as Judas the Galilean had.) Tiberius can have his coins, and he can have his palace. But someday the coins will tarnish, the palace will crumble, and Tiberius will die. Jesus, however, will be King, Son of God, and High Priest for all of eternity.

Jesus did not have political loyalties, we learn in Mark 12. So it can be hard to follow him if you have fierce political loyalties. Jesus is not a liberal, he's not a conservative, and he's not a moderate. So you can't be in one of those categories and say that Jesus is squarely in your category.

This is not to say that Jesus was not political. Jesus was *very* political. He laid out his political vision in Luke 4, where he sets out "to preach good news to the poor . . . to proclaim freedom for the prisoners and recovery of sight for the blind, to release the oppressed." This is not wishy-washy, personal spirituality. This is about changing the world. This is not the cop-out that says that since all politicians are corrupt, all social problems are impossible and you can only mind your own business and worry about your own private affairs. This is the largest-scale social movement in human history.

But the message of Mark 12 is that while Jesus was fundamentally political, he was not *partisan*. He didn't take sides. He didn't accept questions of political policy in the black-and-white, cut-and-dried ways people usually thought about them. He probably wouldn't have had strong feelings about voting for Tiberius or voting for the guy running against Tiberius (if Rome had held elections). And so Christians do a poor imitation of him when they try to claim him for one side against the other, Keller observes. "You must not say, 'That's Jesus' party,' 'That's Jesus' platform,' " Keller says. "Jesus resists political simplicity; he resists being put in a box."

You can tell a lot about Jesus by his request in verse 15, "Bring me a denarius." Not, "Let me pull this denarius out of my pocket and show it to you." Bring me a denarius; I don't have one. Jesus, says Keller, is "a king without a quarter." Tiberius can boast all the wealth of Rome and mint coins from his own stock of silver that bear his name. Jesus doesn't have a quarter to his name. What can we make of this difference?

Keller thinks the answer lies in Luke's account of the Beatitudes in Luke 6. There, Jesus blesses those who lack power, success, wealth, and recognition, and he condemns those who have power, success, wealth, and recognition. To those who lack these four things—the four things Tiberius and everyone in his empire is living for—Jesus says, "Great is your reward in heaven." But to those who, like Tiberius, live to amass more power, success, wealth, and recognition, Jesus says, "You have already received your comfort." You better enjoy what you have, because that's all you get. While Tiberius is living it up in Rome, Jesus will suffer political powerlessness, poverty, obscurity, and eventual execution. All he gets in return is to be King of the universe. While Tiberius, in his vanity, was putting his own face on the quarter, Jesus was making a mark on the world that would never disappear.

This, Keller says, is why Jesus is not another Judas, another revolutionary ranting about Rome, leading revolts, marching around with an army. These revolutions, noble as their intentions may have been, still boiled down to those four things Jesus condemns: power, success, wealth, recognition. Taking power, achieving success, increasing your wealth, enjoying the recognition. These are what revolutionaries live for, and are ready to die for.

The problem is, in their zeal to end the oppression of one group, conventional revolutionaries inevitably end up oppressing another group. And since leaders lust for power (they have a *libido dominandi,* as Augustine put it), they become part of the problem they were revolting against. They abuse their power just like the power abusers they were bent on removing from power. Look at the Marxist revolution of the early twentieth century, for example; it toppled one regime in the name of the people but ended up instituting oppressive Communist autocrats. "Every revolution in the kingdom of the world," Keller says, "is not really changing anything fundamentally, is not really revolutionizing anything. It's just changing the players." It's changing who has the power, success, wealth, and recognition, and who doesn't.

It's ironic that the word *revolution* is what we use to describe the orbit of planets around the sun. *Revolution* means going in circles. It's a coincidence, but it supports what Jesus is saying in Mark 12. Have a revolution, and we'll end up where we started: leaders amassing power, success, wealth, and recognition for themselves and maybe for their followers, but certainly at the expense of someone else. We'll be going in circles.

That's why Jesus refused to be another Judas. He wasn't content to hold a little revolution and lead a little army, because that wouldn't change anything. It would be another power grab in a world full of power grabs. It would be a march for success and recognition in a world where everyone was marching for success and recognition. It would be going in circles. It would be the way of Tiberius, not the way of Jesus. The way of Tiberius doesn't change anything. The way of Jesus changes everything.

That's what N. T. Wright says in stark terms in his teaching on Philippians 3. Paul writes, "But our citizenship is in heaven. And we eagerly await a Savior from there, the Lord Jesus Christ, who by the power that enables him to bring everything under his control, will transform our lowly bodies so that they will be like his glorious body." Wright explains:

> The whole verse says: Jesus is Lord, and Caesar isn't. Caesar's empire, of which Philippi is a colonial outpost, is the parody; Jesus' empire, of which the Philippian church is a colonial outpost, is the reality. And the point of having "citizenship in heaven," as has often been pointed out, is not that one might eventually go home to the mother city; . . . [In Roman times,] the emperor would come from the mother city to rescue and liberate his loyal subjects, transforming their situation from danger to safety.

That's a startling thought—that the kingdom of Tiberius was an unwitting satire, an absurd and flawed imitation of the coming kingdom of Christ. Wright's inspiring conclusion is that Christianity is a "counter-empire" and that the church "can never be merely critical, never merely subversive. It claims to be the reality of which Caesar's empire is the parody; it claims to be modelling the genuine humanness, not least the justice and peace, and the unity across traditional racial and cultural barriers, of which Caesar's empire boasted."

Now we can see why Keller calls Jesus' revolution "a revolution that revolutionizes revolutions." Revolting against the four things everyone in the world lives for—power, success, wealth, and recognition—is about the most radical thing you can do. When you stop living for those four things, you're not living on Tiberius's terms anymore, you're living on God's terms. When you stop living for power, success, wealth, and recognition, then you turn society upside down. Then you minister to the poor, feed the hungry, and pour out yourself in order to be filled up by God and others. If you want to turn the world upside down, then turn your conceptions of—and hope for—power, success, wealth, and recognition upside down.

The Suburban Church of North America

Do Christians do this? Do Christians reject the way of Tiberius Caesar and embrace the way of Jesus Christ? Are Christians visible to the world as a group of people that refuses to play by the world's rules, refuses to chase power, success, wealth, and recognition? Eugene Peterson, in a modern adaptation of the seven letters to churches in the Book of Revelation, answers the question in an article called "To the Suburban Church of North America."

But I have this against you: you're far too impressed with Size and Power and Influence. You are impatient with the small and the slow. You exercise little discernment between the ways of the world and my ways. It distresses me that you so uncritically copy the attitudes and methods that make your life in suburbia work so well. You grab onto anything that works and looks good. You do many good things, but too often you do them in the world's way instead of mine, and so you seriously compromise your obedience.

The problem, writes William Romanowski, is that American Christians are too content and comfortable living by the ways of their country. "Like most Americans, they tend to privatize their faith, confining religion to family and local congregation, while conducting their affairs in business, politics, education, social life, and the arts much like everyone else." We have lost sight of the reality Madeleine L'Engle speaks to when she says, "Jesus was a great universe-disturber. Those of us who try to follow his Way have a choice, either to go with him as universe-disturbers or to play it safe."

Many American Christians opt to play it safe. The American church doesn't seem very uncomfortable coexisting with the American state. There isn't much disturbing going on.

What we need is what Walter Brueggemann calls *exilic consciousness*—the awareness that we are exiled under a foreign empire to which our ultimate allegiance does not belong. This is how the exiles of Judah lived when their kingdom fell into the hands of King Nebuchadnezzar and the Chaldeans. Like them, Brueggemann says, American Christians have to develop a "deep sense of displacement . . . [in] the place where the faithful church must now live."

How does this work? How can Christians live in America and call themselves Americans and yet have a deep sense of displacement? How can we be natives and foreigners at the same time? Daniel Jurman sheds some light on this dilemma in his play *In a Den of Lions*, which portrays the life of Daniel and his Judean friends among the Chaldeans in Babylon.

Growing up, I thought of Daniel as the one who was miraculously rescued from the lions' den and whose friends were rescued from the fiery furnace, but I was mostly oblivious to the cultural context in which these miracles took place. Daniel and his friends were in an incredibly awkward position. They had been handpicked by Nebuchadnezzar's palace master, Ashpenaz, to serve in Nebuchadnezzar's palace. The Book of Daniel is the story of how these four men had to live amid a pagan empire and serve it while retaining their loyalty to God. At any given moment, they risked offending Nebuchadnezzar and losing their position, or selling out to the establishment and dropping their faith.

In his play, Jurman suggests the ground rules the four friends laid for themselves. Jurman opens with Ashpenaz conducting an initial examination of Daniel and his friends, boldly vowing that "when we are finished with these men of Judah, they will be Chaldeans in mind, body and soul." Jurman imagines Daniel conferring with his friends afterward and wondering how to be a Chaldean who believes in God. Finally Daniel makes a declaration: "In every way that is unimportant, let them make us Chaldeans," he says. "Let them change our names and teach us their culture if that makes them comfortable. But let us teach them as well. Let us teach them what it is to be faithful to the one true Lord of all."

This is a good rule of thumb for Christians in America, living in a society that is out to make us Americans in mind, body, and soul. In every way that is unimportant, let them make us Americans. Let them teach us their culture. But let us teach them as well. Let us appear to be Americans, but deep down, let us be different.

It sounds simple, but of course the crucial question is which American ways are unimportant and which are important. This is what Christians must constantly discuss. Clothes, food, and language are probably not that important. American practices of self-worship, hoarding wealth, recreational sex with strangers, and military domination *are* important.

Like Daniel in the Chaldean empire, and Jesus in the Roman Empire, we live in the midst of a worldly kingdom, and we're stuck with it. We cannot withdraw like the Essenes or try to overthrow it like the Zealots. But we must constantly check ourselves on whether we are conforming to the worldly kingdom in important ways and not just trivial ones. After all, this worldly kingdom is not our home; we belong in an eternal kingdom that Jesus planted and is coming back to harvest. D. Brent Laytham strings together a stirring series of adjectives to make the point: "However it might be with other gods, to serve this God is a community-enfolding, life-encompassing, allegiance-demanding whole. When Yahweh says, 'I am your God,' it is an invitation to the freedom of absolute allegiance." Half-hearted Christianity and cultural conformity won't cut it.

After Daniel and the Judeans were carted off to Babylon, the prophet Jeremiah sent them a letter. He gave them God's command for how to live in their new surroundings. We tend to think of Jeremiah as a complainer, a prophet whose prophecies were almost always dismal; we even call a rant or complaint a "jeremiad." But one particular passage in Jeremiah 29 is especially uplifting. Jeremiah passes along God's instructions that the exiles should build houses and have families in Babylon, and not just sit there and mope. Then he gives them a memorable order: "Seek the peace and prosperity [the Hebrew is *shalom*] of the city to which I have carried you into exile. Pray to the LORD for it, because if it prospers, you too will prosper." Three verses later, God promises to bring everyone back to Jerusalem. And then, in verse 11, he makes this sweet promise: " 'For I know the plans I have for you,' declares the LORD, 'plans to prosper you and not to harm you, plans to give you hope and a future.' "

Many people misuse verse 11, taking it out of context and using it to assure themselves that God promises worldly prosperity to everyone he loves. But the context, and God's "plans," are clear: they are an assurance to people in exile that God-with-us will be restored, that although they are foreigners now, some-day they will be home, in Jerusalem, where they belong. This is how we should hear Jeremiah's prophecy: not as a generic state-ment of optimism but as a promise to us, who are exiled amid a worldly kingdom, that someday we, too, will be home.

Sojourning Strangers

Until then, we struggle with our status as "aliens and strangers in the world," as 1 Peter 2 puts it. Stanley Hauerwas's term for Christians is "resident aliens," echoing an anonymous second-century letter writer to a man named Diognetus. The letter said: "They reside in their own countries, but only as alien citizens, and endure everything as foreigners. Every foreign country is their homeland, and every homeland a foreign country. . . . Chris-tians live in the world, but are not of the world." If we aren't sticking out somehow, then chances are we're doing something wrong.

Maybe the proper metaphor, as proposed by Laura Smit, is that Christian citizens are *ambassadors*. The ambassador to France, for instance, lives in France, speaks French, eats French cuisine, and desires the prosperity of France. But she remains a foreigner. The national anthem of France will never roll off her lips so naturally as it does for a French citizen. So it is with the church in America and Canada. We live here, eat the food, sing the national anthem, and even, when its cause is just, die for our nation in battle. But we will never truly belong to our country the way we belong to the church. Like ambassadors, we are representatives of another kingdom, another set of allegiances. Like ambassadors, our goal is the mutual benefit of the two kingdoms between which we are some sort of a bridge. But all the while, our faith never wavers that our true kingdom will one day prevail, and that only then we will be home and no longer foreigners. Wright has a fine phrase for the apostle Paul and his missionary activity. Paul, Wright says, was "an ambassador for a king-in-waiting." So are we.

Despite our dueling allegiances, we do not wish ill on the land in which we are exiled. God did say in Jeremiah 29, after all, to "work for the peace and prosperity of the city" in which we are in exile. We cannot withhold our loyalty, superficial as it is, to our country. Nor can we sit around and wait for the completion of God's eternal kingdom. We cannot hide from Caesar as the Essenes did, or fight him as the Zealots did. We have to work for the good of the worldly kingdom in which we are in exile. This gets tricky when the good of our worldly kingdom conflicts with the good of the eternal kingdom, and the latter must always win out over the former for us. But as Daniel proved, working for a worldly kingdom with an unshakeable allegiance to a heavenly kingdom can be done, very carefully, with God's grace.

So we're supposed to stand out and not fit in. We're supposed to squirm a little in our social surroundings, to be uncomfortable with the worldly ways around us rather than get used to them. "Do not conform any longer to the pattern of this world," Paul says, "but be transformed by the renewing of your mind." He says this in chapter 12 of his letter to the church in Tiberius's hometown, Rome. Eugene Peterson has a handy paraphrase of this passage: "Don't become so well adjusted to your culture that you fit into it without thinking."

This is not to suggest that, for all Jesus' words of warning about the ways of Tiberius—power, wealth, success, and recognition—these things are always evil. They can be false gods, but they can also be false *idols* when we assume that anyone who has these four things is automatically ungodly and anyone who lacks them is automatically godly. The message of Jesus' kingdom is this: Placing these four things as our ultimate goals, our driving ambitions, our reasons for living, our justification for mistreating others—this is the way of Tiberius. It is possible, through God's grace, to be blessed with the benefits of worldly power, wealth, success, and recognition and still be faithful to the heavenly kingdom. At times, these four things can even be used to help the kingdom come "a little more." But they are not our reasons for being.

In his service to the Chaldeans, Daniel had all the power, wealth, success, and recognition a person could want, but he risked it all, and his very life, when he was given the choice: bow to the Chaldean king or be served as midnight snack to a den of hungry lions. Daniel never batted an eye. We think of God's miraculous intervention in shutting the mouths of the lions around Daniel as God's blessing on a righteous man, but more specifically, it is God's blessing on a *loyal* man. We must be just as loyal; we must do what some of us sang in Sunday school:

177

"Dare to Be a Daniel." Like Daniel, we must have the courage to maintain a loyalty that goes deeper than the question of whose national anthem we sing but is imprinted on our personhood.

"Imprinted" is an apt word. Notice, Keller says, that to set up his answer in Mark 12, Jesus asked whose picture was on the denarius. The coins bore the image of Caesar, so they were to be given to him. We bear the image of God, so our lives must be given to him.

Sojourning Servants

The choice to reject power, wealth, success, and recognition as inherently important is not an easy one. That's the lesson of the life of Jesus. Tiberius had it made, for his brief life. Jesus had it hellish but is exalted for eternity. To be like Jesus, then, is to reject the way of Tiberius in favor of storing up treasures in a heavenly kingdom. The way of Jesus, writes Quentin Schultze, "emphasizes selfless servanthood rather than selfish masterhood," in which "*Masterhood* is selfish domination of others. *Servanthood* is humble service to our neighbor." As a result, Schultze says, invoking the term of the priest Henri Nouwen, we must pursue *downward mobility*.

After all, "Christ did not exploit his status for selfish purposes. Instead, Christ 'humbled himself' (Phil 2:8). He took the position of a mere human being." So to imitate Christ means to imitate his downward mobility. Jesus said it himself in the story about the sheep and the goats in Matthew 25. He tells those who enter into eternal life, "I was hungry and you gave me something to eat, I was thirsty and you gave me something to drink, I was a stranger and you invited me in, I needed clothes and you clothed me, I was sick and you looked after me, I was in prison and you came to visit me." The saints do not remember seeing him this way, but Jesus says, "Whatever you did for one of the least of these brothers and sisters of mine, you did for me." Ronald Sider reads this passage and writes, in *Rich Christians in an Age of Hunger*: "What does it mean to feed and clothe the Creator of all things? We cannot know. We can only look at the poor and oppressed with new eyes and resolve to heal their hurts and help end their oppression."

Upward mobility is the way of Tiberius. Like him, you chase power, wealth, success, and recognition with all your might, with little regard to your relationships with people other than how you can exploit them, and no regard to the disenfranchised, since they lack the four things you're living for. And then you die, and those four things are worthless. (Historians say Tiberius died ignobly; terminally ill, he was smothered with a pillow by his servants in order to speed up the coronation of his successor.) But people who reject the fundamental ideal of upward mobility receive the blessings described in that letter to Diognetus, with its echoes of Jesus' Beatitudes: "They are put to death, yet are more alive than ever. They are paupers, but they make many rich. They lack all things, and yet in all things they abound." Chase upward mobility to the exclusion of all else, and you enjoy it only until you die. Seek Christ-like downward mobility, and you are resurrected to eternal life in heaven. Downward mobility is upward mobility toward heaven.

The shallow understanding of religion in our society is this: do good works so you can go to heaven. When Homer Simpson finds himself before Saint Peter at the pearly gates on *The Simpsons*, Peter tells him he must return to earth and do a good deed before he can get in. (When Homer does, Peter says he wasn't watching.) Heaven is a reward for being nice.

But the truth of Christianity is this: you are given eternal life by grace, and doing good now testifies to the reality of the coming eternal kingdom of God. Being Christ-like is fundamentally *anticipatory*; it hints at something to come, its presence suggests the future. It is like the series of notes in an orchestra piece that swell and build toward the resolution of that final, perfect chord. You can almost hear the chord before it's played, and when it's finally struck, it is all the more satisfying because of the notes that led up to it. It wouldn't be the same if the orchestra sat down and played that final chord alone.

The fruit of the Spirit of Galatians 5 is like the closing measures of a symphony, building toward a final resolution. The meaning of love, joy, peace, patience, kindness, goodness, faithfulness, gentleness, and self-control is this: we are destined for a new earth on which these fruits will grow and flourish in perpetuity. These virtues are good in themselves, but their beauty lies in part in the future they imply. Embodying them now does not just make you nice and agreeable; it makes you a walking testimony to the fact that heaven is on the way. As Lewis Smedes beautifully put it, being like Christ means "living the sort of life that makes people say, 'Ah, so that's how people are going to live when righteousness takes over our world.'"

Peter—the real Saint Peter, not the one in the *Simpsons* cartoon—says the same thing in 2 Peter 3: "In keeping with his promise we are looking forward to a new heaven and a new earth, the home of righteousness. So then, dear friends, since you are looking forward to this, make every effort to be found spotless, blameless, and at peace with him." So then, *since* you are looking forward to this, be righteous. Be found spotless for a purpose.

This verse comes directly after Peter's prophecy of the new earth, as examined in chapter 3. Peter could have ended by saying, "That's what will happen; just wanted to let you know what was coming." Instead he ties his vision of the end to living a Christ-like life. And not just as a contingency plan—be good or get burned. His vision is one of congruence: make a connection to heaven now, already, before it comes. Find a pattern of continuity to the ways of the coming kingdom, and live it out in the current kingdom. Do your best to live like Christ, because this is a dress rehearsal for the big show, when Christ returns.

Earlier I mentioned Richard Mouw's concerns about the perspective of the famous allegory *The Pilgrim's Progress*. The metaphor, as he pointed out, goes only so far. The Christian life is not a solitary journey to a remote location. Nonetheless, we can recover some parts of the classic allegory in order to deepen our understanding of our current age and how it is leading to the eternal age of heaven.

The Christian life is, at some times and in some ways, like a journey, a pilgrimage along a path to the celestial city. We are indeed going somewhere, and we are indeed not there yet. Schultze explains this metaphor well:

> We recognize that the current world is not fully home; it is not a perfect fit for the shalom we desire. Nevertheless, this world is the place where our journey occurs. Here we discover where we are from as well as evidence of the things to come. We sojourn in a "now" that is informed by wisdom from the past and directed by desires for . . . an eternal future that we can barely perceive through the shadows of time.

The purpose of this book is to make us feel *more* at home and *less* at home. More at home because the Bible says our eternal life will somehow resemble our current life more than we tend to think—it will be on earth, in human bodies, among culture, and in relationships. Our current lives, and the things that make up our current existence, are not just temporary distractions before an eternity of fluttering about on clouds. All of these things—the earth, our bodies, human culture, and our relationships—are a sneak preview of heaven. Realizing this is how we understand the essence of those things in this present age. Presuming these things are irrelevant empties our current existence of meaning and purpose.

But this book is also written to make us feel less at home. The message of heaven is, after all, supposed to make us long for that better place. The promise of heaven is intended to make us itch for heaven, thirst for it, long for it, to have a holy restlessness as we live our current lives. The promise of heaven is the alternative to our culture's fatuous attempts to explain the meaning of life: that life is one big chase for things or one selfish grab for power, wealth, success, and recognition. Life means so much more, because heaven will be so much more. And so we should live with daily discomfort about the fact that we are not yet in heaven, and let this plant hope in our hearts that someday we will be.

I began with the last words of Henry Thoreau. On his deathbed, he said, "One world at a time, Parker, one world at a time." I said the purpose of this book is to show that Thoreau was wrong. He was not wrong to say that the end of this life is the official entry to the next—it is. But in another sense, we live in two worlds at once, the already and the not yet, our present shaped by the future. We run now because the finish line is coming later, and running a race that is not directed toward the finish line is a meaningless exercise, a waste of breath.

Without hope for heaven, our lives are limp and empty. But we have the Bible's promise that God will one day restore planet earth to the full flourishing it was intended to have, will restore the works of human minds and hands to again give glory to him alone, and will restore human relationships with others and with himself to their fullest expression. Creation will again sing with the harmony of *shalom*, the way things are supposed to be. This is how we understand how and why we are alive, why we do the things we do, why we know sorrow and joy in this age. Someday God will wipe every tear from our eyes and unveil the boundless glory of all that he has made. This is the promise of heaven. This is the hope of our lives.

And so our last words can only be the same ones John says at the end of Revelation 22, the last words of the Bible before its closing benediction. John writes, "He who testifies to these things says, 'Yes, I am coming soon.' " We echo John's response.

"Amen. Come, Lord Jesus."

REFERENCES

Page numbers of quotations from the following sources and suggestions for further reading are available at www.nbierma.com /heaven.

Chapter 1: Lost in the Cornfield: Hope in Crisis

Associated Press, June 28, 1981; September 13, 1988; January 9, 1999. (Reports of false alarms.)

Clouse, Robert J., Robert N. Hosack, and Richard V. Pierard. *The New Millennium Manual.* Grand Rapids, Mich.: BridgePoint Books, 1999.

Franklin, Stephen. "Running Faster Just to Fall Further Behind." *Chicago Tribune*, September 15, 2002.

Keats quoted in Lewis, "The Weight of Glory."

Kraybill, J. Nelson. "Apocalypse Now." *Christianity Today*, October 25, 1999.

Lamott, Anne. *Traveling Mercies: Some Thoughts on Faith.* New York: Anchor, 1999.

Leland, John. "Heaven Comes Down to Earth." *New York Times*, December 21, 2003.

Lewis, C. S., on "mudpies" and "chills, rather than awakes" in "The Weight of Glory." Sermon, the Church of St. Mary the Virgin, Oxford, England, June 8, 1941; reprinted in *The Weight of Glory and Other Addresses*. Grand Rapids, Mich.: Eerdmans, 1965. On "laying eggs" in *Mere Christianity*. San Francisco: Harper, 1952.

Miller, Lisa. "Why We Need Heaven." *Newsweek*, August 12, 2002.

Moltmann, Jurgen. *Theology of Hope*. New York: Harper & Row, 1967.

Mouw, Richard. *When the Kings Come Marching In: Isaiah and the New Jerusalem*. Grand Rapids, Mich.: Eerdmans, 2002.

Plantinga, Cornelius J. "In the Interim." Sermon, St. Olaf College, Northfield, Minn., July 24, 2000; accessed at <http://www.religion-online.org/showarticle.asp?title=2020>.

"Quo Vadimus" (Season 2, Episode 22, #45, code N-345). *Sports-Night*, ABC, May 16, 2000.

Roberts, Arthur O. *Exploring Heaven: What Great Christian Thinkers Tell Us about Our Afterlife with God*. San Francisco: HarperSanFrancisco, 2003.

Rushin, Steve. *Road Swing*. New York: Doubleday, 1998. Description of Dyersville, Iowa.

Schor, Juliet. *The Overworked American: The Unexpected Decline of Leisure*. New York: Basic Books, 1992.

Smedes, Lewis B. *How Can It Be All Right When Everything Is All Wrong?* San Francisco: Harper & Row, 1982.

Turner, Dale. "Year after Year, Easter Resurrects Worshipers' Hopes for Eternal Life." *The Seattle Times*, April 3, 1999.

VanderKlippe, Nathan. E-mail to author. January 1, 2003.

Weiss, Jeffrey. "What's the Afterlife Like?" *Dallas Morning News*, November 1, 2003.

"What Heaven Must Taste Like." America Online, "Welcome" screen, December 8, 2004.

Willimon quoted in Plantinga.

Yancey, Philip. *I Was Just Wondering*. Grand Rapids, Mich.: Eerdmans, 1989. In "Whatever Happened to Heaven?"

Chapter 2: On Purpose: Meaning in Crisis

"Blood Feud" (7F22). *The Simpsons*, Fox, July 11, 1991.

Dark, David. *Everyday Apocalypse: The Sacred Revealed in Radiohead, The Simpsons, and Other Pop Culture Icons.* Grand Rapids, Mich.: Brazos Press, 2002.

de Graaf, John, et al. *Affluenza: The All-Consuming Epidemic.* San Francisco: Berrett-Koehler, 2001.

Erb, Paul. *The Alpha and the Omega: A Restatement of the Christian Hope in Christ's Coming.* Scottdale, Pa.: Herald Press, 1955.

Garber, Steven. *The Fabric of Faithfulness.* Downers Grove, Ill.: InterVarsity Press, 1996.

L'Engle, Madeleine. *The Irrational Season.* New York: Seabury Press, 1976.

The Matrix. Directed by Andy and Larry Wachowski. Warner Brothers, 1999.

Muggeridge quoted in bulletin, Fourth Presbyterian Church, Chicago, October 20, 2002.

Murray, Donald M. *Writing for Your Readers: Notes on the Writer's Craft from the Boston Globe.* Old Saybrook, Conn.: Globe Pequot Press, 1992.

Quindlen, Anna. "Honestly, You Shouldn't Have." *Newsweek*, December 3, 2001.

Pahl, Jon. *Shopping Malls and Other Sacred Spaces.* Grand Rapids, Mich.: Brazos Press, 2003.

Reality Bites. Directed by Ben Stiller. Universal Pictures, 1994.

Roosevelt and Thanksgiving discussed in Boorstin, Daniel J. *The Americans: The Democratic Experience.* New York: Vintage, 1974.

Schor, Juliet. *The Overspent American: Why We Want What We Don't Need.* New York: HarperPerennial, 1999.

Scott, A. O. "Vaulting Ambivalence." *New York Times*, November 10, 2002.

Smith, Gordon T. *Courage and Calling: Embracing Your God-Given Potential.* Downers Grove, Ill.: InterVarsity Press, 1999.

Twitchell, James. *Lead Us into Temptation: The Triumph of American Materialism.* New York: Columbia University Press, 1999.

Winter, Richard. *Still Bored in a Culture of Entertainment: Rediscovering Passion and Wonder.* Downers Grove, Ill.: InterVarsity Press, 2002.

Zaleski quoted in Roberts, Arthur O. *Exploring Heaven.* See chapter 1 references.

Chapter 3: Theater of Glory: Heaven on Earth

"The Beginning Is Near" in advertisement for "Origins." *Nova*, PBS, September 28–29, 2004.

Brueggemann, Walter. "Environment as Creation." *Books & Culture*, January/February 2004.

Calvin quoted in Schreiner, Susan. *The Theater of His Glory: Nature and the Natural Order in the Thought of John Calvin.* Grand Rapids, Mich.: Baker Academic, 2001.

Chesterton, G. K. quoted in Yancey, Philip. *Soul Survivor: How My Faith Survived the Church.* New York: Doubleday, 2001.

Dyrness, William A. *The Earth Is God's: A Theology of American Culture.* New York: Orbis Books, 1997.

Gushee, David P. "When Marriage Brings Suffering." *Books & Culture*, September/October 2004.

Griffiths, Jay. *A Sideways Look at Time.* New York: Jeremy P. Tarcher, 2004.

Hendra, Tony. *Father Joe.* Quoted in bulletin, Fourth Presbyterian Church, Chicago, June 27, 2004.

Hoekema, Anthony. *The Bible and the Future.* Grand Rapids, Mich.: Eerdmans, 1979.

Hoezee, Scott. *Remember Creation: God's World of Wonder and Delight.* Grand Rapids, Mich.: Eerdmans, 1998.

Keizer, Garret. "Faith, Hope, and Ecology." *Christian Century*, December 5, 2001.

Kristof, Nicholas. "Dare We Call It Genocide?" *New York Times*, June 16, 2004.

Lamott, Anne. *Bird by Bird: Some Instructions on Writing and Life.* New York: Anchor, 1995.

Lemonick, Michael D. "Life in the Greenhouse." *Time*, April 9, 2001.

Miller, Vassar. *Struggling to Swim on Concrete*. New Orleans: New Orleans Poetry Journal Press, 1984. "Morning Person." Used with permission.

Paton quoted in Fosdick, Harry Emerson. *The Meaning of Prayer*. Quoted in bulletin, LaSalle Street Church, Chicago, June 20, 2004.

Plantinga, Cornelius. *Not the Way It's Supposed to Be: A Breviary of Sin*. Grand Rapids, Mich.: Eerdmans, 1995.

Richards, Larry. *Zondervan Dictionary of Christian Literacy: Key Concepts of the Faith*. Grand Rapids, Mich.: Zondervan, 1990.

Van Dyke, Fred, David C. Mahan, Joseph K. Sheldon, and Raymond H. Brand. *Redeeming Creation: The Biblical Basis for Environmental Stewardship*. Downers Grove, Ill.: InterVarsity Press, 1996.

von Rad, Gerhard. *Wisdom in Israel*. Quoted at weblog, Gideon Strauss. Accessed at <www.gideonstrauss.com>.

Willimon, William H. *Sighing for Eden: Sin, Evil, and the Christian Faith*. Nashville: Abingdon, 1985.

Wittmer, Michael. *Heaven Is a Place on Earth: Why Everything You Do Matters to God*. Grand Rapids, Mich.: Zondervan, 2004.

Wolters, Al on 2 Peter 3 in "Worldview and Textual Criticism in 2 Peter 3:10." *Westminster Theological Journal* 49 (1987): 405–13; on "the works of the craftsman's art" in *Creation Regained: Biblical Basics of a Reformational Worldview*. Grand Rapids, Mich.: Eerdmans, 1985.

Chapter 4: Beating Our Swords: The Greatest Commission

Brown, Robert McAfee. *Spirituality and Liberation*. Quoted in bulletin, Fourth Presbyterian Church, Chicago, July 11, 2004.

Casablanca. Directed by Michael Curtiz. Warner Brothers, 1942.

Cronon, William. *Nature's Metropolis: Chicago and the Great West*. New York: Norton, 1992.

Dyrness, William. *The Earth Is God's*. See chapter 3 references.

Lewis, C. S. "The Weight of Glory." See chapter 1 references.

Mouw, Richard J. *When the Kings Come Marching In.* See chapter 1 references. On "nothing is wasted" in interview with the author, January 2003.

Peterson, Eugene. "Following Caiaphas: The Successful Leader." McCormick Theological Seminary, Chicago, September 26, 2003.

Plantinga, Cornelius. *A Sure Thing: What We Believe and Why.* Grand Rapids, Mich.: CRC Publications, 1986.

Roberts, Arthur O. *Exploring Heaven.* See chapter 1 references.

Schultze, Quentin J. *Communicating for Life: Christian Stewardship in Community and Media.* Grand Rapids, Mich.: Baker Academic, 2000.

Smit, Laura. Religion 301. Christianity and Culture. Course, Calvin College, Grand Rapids, Mich., spring 2001.

VanderKlippe, Nathan. E-mail to author. January 1, 2003.

Wittmer, Michael. *Heaven Is a Place on Earth.* See chapter 3 references.

Chapter 5: Nurseries of Virtue: Urban Heaven

Augustine. *On the Two Cities: Selections from The City of God.* Edited by F. W. Strothmann. New York: Ungar, 1957.

Franzen, Jonathan. *How to Be Alone: Essays.* New York: Farrar, Straus and Giroux, 2002.

Goldberg quoted at Great Buildings Online. Accessed at <http://www.greatbuildings.com/buildings/Marina_City.html>.

Gorringe, T. J. *A Theology of the Built Environment: Justice, Empowerment, Redemption.* New York: Cambridge University Press, 2002.

Jacobsen, Eric O. *Sidewalks in the Kingdom: New Urbanism and the Christian Faith.* Grand Rapids, Mich.: Brazos Press, 2003.

Kamin, Blair. *Why Architecture Matters: Lessons from Chicago.* Chicago: University of Chicago Press, 2001.

Mouw, Richard J. *When the Kings Come Marching In.* See chapter 1 references.

Rykwert, Joseph. *The Seduction of Place: The History and Future of the City.* New York: Vintage, 2002.

Chapter 6: Future Presence: God with Us

Augustine. *Confessions.* Translated with introduction by R. S Pine-Coffin. London: Penguin, 1961.

Buechner, Frederick. *Beyond Words: Daily Readings in the ABCs of Faith.* New York: HarperCollins, 2004. On "death-proof" in "Immortality." On "too good not to be true" in "Eve."

Fairchild quoted in Hankins, Barry. "Lonesome Blues." *Books & Culture*, September/October 2003.

Hendra, Tony. *Father Joe.* Quoted in bulletin, Fourth Presbyterian Church, Chicago, June 27, 2004.

Keller, Timothy, on relationship with God in "Arguing about the Afterlife." Sermon, Redeemer Presbyterian Church, New York City, July 1, 2001. On "the image of an us" in "God with Us." Sermon, Redeemer Presbyterian Church, New York City, November 10, 2002.

Kushner quoted in Kuyvenhoven, Len. "Getting Ready: Part 3—Rejoice." Sermon, Neland Avenue Christian Reformed Church, Grand Rapids, Mich., December 12, 2004.

Lamott, Anne. *Traveling Mercies.* See chapter 1 references.

Laytham, D. Brent, ed. *God Is Not: Religious, Nice, One of Us, an American, a Capitalist.* Grand Rapids, Mich.: Brazos Press, 2004.

Lewis, C. S. "The Weight of Glory." See chapter 1 references.

Merton, Thomas, *New Seeds of Contemplation.* New York: New Directions Publishing, 1972.

Sartre quoted in Tournier.

Simon and Garfunkel. "A Most Peculiar Man." *Sounds of Silence.* Sony, 1966.

Stratman, Deborah. Interview with the author, September 6, 2004.

Tournier, Paul. *The Meaning of Persons.* New York: Harper & Row, 1957.

Truax, Laura. "The Eighth Day." Sermon, LaSalle Street Church, Chicago, May 23, 2004.

Wesley quoted in Mouw, Richard J., and Mark A. Noll, eds. *Wonderful Words of Life: Hymns in American Protestant History and Theology.* Grand Rapids, Mich.: Eerdmans, 2004.

Yancey, Philip. *Reaching for the Invisible God: What Can We Expect to Find?* Grand Rapids, Mich.: Zondervan, 2000.

Chapter 7: Thinking Big: Connecting Heavenly Hope to Daily Life

Bierma, William. Unpublished and untitled memoirs.

Buechner, Frederick. *Beyond Words.* See chapter 6 references. On "deep hunger" in "Vocation."

Buning, Sietze. *Style and Class.* Orange City, Iowa: Middleburg Press, 1982.

Byker, Gaylen. "What's a Christian Worldview For?" Convocation address, Calvin College, Grand Rapids, Mich., September 4, 2001.

Cullmann quoted in Hoekema.

Dark, David. *Everyday Apocalypse.* See chapter 2 references.

Dill, Carl, on servant leadership, interview with the author, October 2001. Dill's experiences described in Mouw, Richard, "He Shines in All That's Fair: Culture and Common Grace." The Stob Lectures, Calvin College, October 2000.

Garber, Steven. *The Fabric of Faithfulness.* See chapter 2 references.

Gunther, Marc. "God and Business." *Fortune*, July 9, 2001.

Hoekema, Anthony. *The Bible and the Future.* See chapter 3 references.

Humanist Manifesto, quoted and critiqued in *Our World Belongs to God: A Contemporary Testimony: Study Edition.* Grand Rapids, Mich.: CRC Publications, 1987.

"I'll Fly Away" in Alison Krauss and Gillian Welch. "I'll Fly Away." *O Brother, Where Art Thou? Music from a Film by Joel Coen and Ethan Coen.* Lost Highway, 2000.

Lewis, C. S. quoted in Loconte, Joseph. "A Mind That Grasped Both Heaven and Hell." *New York Times*, November 23, 2003.

Lopez quoted in "Lopez's Ladder of Love." *The Week*, December 2, 2002.

Luther quoted in Marshall.

Kuyper quoted and discussed in Mouw, Richard. *Calvinism in the Las Vegas Airport.* Kuyper's change of beliefs about the resurrection in

Schaap, James C. *No Kidding, God*. Grand Rapids, Mich.: CRC Publications, 1990. In "Meditation 5: Dominion."

Marshall in Noll, Mark, and David Wells, eds. *Christian Faith and Practice in the Modern World*. In Marshall, Paul, "Calling, Work and Rest." Grand Rapids, Mich.: Eerdmans, 1981.

Maxwell quoted in "All Things." Calvin College admissions office, 2002.

McCarthy, David Matzko. *The Good Life: Genuine Christianity for the Middle Class*. Grand Rapids, Mich.: Brazos Press, 2004.

Mouw, Richard, on "personal transaction" and "it is well with my soul" in *When the Kings Come Marching In: Isaiah 60 and the New Jerusalem*. See chapter 4 references.

Miller, Arthur F. *Why You Can't Be Anything You Want to Be*. Grand Rapids, Mich.: Zondervan, 1999.

Price, Robert M. "The Personal Savior: Reclaiming the Language of Piety." *The Reformed Journal*, August 1981.

Retirement, "Golden Years," AIG Sun retirement consulting online, accessed spring 2002 at <www.visualize-retirement.com>.

Retirement home sign seen in "Bart vs. Thanksgiving" (7F07). *The Simpsons*, Fox, November 22, 1990.

Romanowski, William. *Eyes Wide Open: Looking for God in Popular Culture*. Grand Rapids, Mich.: Brazos Press, 2001.

Schultze, Quentin, on televangelism in *Redeeming Television*. Downers Grove, Ill.: InterVarsity Press, 1992; on the theology of communication in *Communicating for Life*. See chapter 4 references.

Steven Garber, *Fabric of Faithfulness*. See chapter 2 references.

"Sunday Protestant" in "Take the Deviled Eggs" (Season 3, Episode 6; #49). *Gilmore Girls*, WB Network, November 5, 2002.

Van Der Weele, Steve. *Neland News*, Neland Avenue Christian Reformed Church, Grand Rapids, Mich., September 12, 2004. Review of Schuurman, Douglas J., *Vocation: Discerning Our Callings in Life*. Grand Rapids, Mich.: Eerdmans, 2004.

Wittmer, Michael. *Heaven Is a Place on Earth*. See chapter 1 references.

Worldview, criticism of, discussed in Siedell, Daniel. "A New View of Worldview." *Books & Culture* online, August 18, 2003. Review of Naugle, David, *Worldview: The History of a Concept.*

Wright, N. T. "Paul's Gospel and Caesar's Empire." *Reflections* 2 (1998). Accessed at <http://www.ctinquiry.org/publications/reflections_volume_2/download_volume_2/wright_essay.pdf>.

Chapter 8: Alien Ambassadors: Living as Citizens of Heaven

Brueggemann, Walter. *Cadences of Home: Preaching among Exiles.* Louisville: Westminster John Knox Press, 1997.

Garber, Steven. "Worship, Worldview, and Way of Life." Calvin Symposium on Worship and the Arts, Calvin Institute of Christian Worship, Grand Rapids, Mich., January 31, 2004.

Jurman, Daniel. "In a Den of Lions: The Life of Daniel in Exile." Unpublished, performed at First Presbyterian Church, Clayton, New Jersey, 1995.

Keller, Timothy. "Arguing about Politics." Sermon, Redeemer Presbyterian Church, New York City, July 15, 2001.

Lamott, Anne. *Traveling Mercies.* See chapter 1 references.

L'Engle, Madeleine. *A Stone for a Pillow.* Quoted in bulletin, Fourth Presbyterian Church, Chicago, November 17, 2002.

Letter to Diognetus quoted in Laytham, D. Brent, ed. *God Is Not: Religious, Nice, One of Us, an American, a Capitalist.* Grand Rapids, Mich.: Brazos Press, 2004. In Baxter, Michael J. "God Is Not an American."

Peterson, Eugene. "To the Suburban Church of North America." *Christianity Today*, October 25, 1999.

Romanowski, William. *Eyes Wide Open: Looking for God in Popular Culture.* See chapter 7 references.

Schultze on downward mobility in *Communicating for Life*; see chapter 4 references. On sojourning in *Habits of the High-Tech Heart: Living Virtuously in the Information Age.* Grand Rapids, Mich.: Baker Academic, 2002.

Smedes, Lewis. *Standing on the Promises*, quoted in Plantinga, "In the Interim." See chapter 1 references.

REFERENCES

Smit, Laura. Religion 301: Christianity and Culture. See chapter 4 references.

Tiberius Caesar's coin inscription quoted in Keller and "Coins of the New Testament," Classical Coins online. Accessed at <http://www.classicalcoins.com/page75.html>.

Tiberius Caesar's death recounted in "Tiberius," Daily Bible Study of Key-Way Publishing, Burford, Ontario. Accessed at <http://www.keyway.ca/htm2002/tiberius.htm>.

"Tree House of Horror XI" (BABF21). *The Simpsons*, Fox, November 1, 2000.

Wall Street. Directed by Oliver Stone. 20th Century Fox, 1987.

Wright, N. T., "Paul's Gospel and Caesar's Empire." See chapter 7 references.

INDEX OF SUBJECTS AND NAMES

Nathan L. K. Bierma is a Christian journalist who seeks to bridge the gap between academia and popular culture. He graduated from Calvin College, where he also teaches English, and is Communications and Research Coordinator at the Calvin Institute of Christian Worship. Reflecting his widespread interests in the arts, media, and culture, Bierma is a contributing features writer for the *Chicago Tribune* and contributing editor to *Books & Culture* magazine.